# RATIONAL  MADNESS
## The Paradox of Addiction

## Ray Hoskins

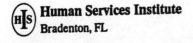
**Human Services Institute**
Bradenton, FL

**TAB BOOKS Inc.**
Blue Ridge Summit, PA

Library of Congress Cataloging in Publication Data

Hoskins, Ray.
    Rational madness.

    Bibliography: p.
    Includes index.
    1. Compulsive behavior.    2. Substance abuse—Treat-
ment.    I. Title.
RC533.H67        1989              616.86          88-38256
ISBN 0-8306-8001-2
ISBN 0-8306-9201-0 (pbk.)

Questions regarding the content of this book should be addressed
to:

Human Services Institute, Inc.
P.O. Box 14610
Bradenton, FL 34280

Development Editor: Lee Marvin Joiner, Ph.D.

TAB BOOKS Inc. offers software for sale. For information and
a catalog, please contact TAB Software Department, Blue Ridge
Summit, PA 17294-0850.

Cover photograph by Susan Riley, Harrisonburg, VA.

*Dedicated to*

***Leona Hoskins-Shapcott and William Manzenberger,***

*my grandparents and early advisors.*

## Disclaimer

Both the author and publisher advise the reader that no mental health treatment is offered in this book. Reading this book is not an alternative to, or substitute for, seeking the help of a professional if you have an addiction problem.

# CONTENTS

Gaining Perspective. Stalking the Perfect Orgasm. Coping with the Symptoms. What is Addictive Process? Security, Sensation, and Power. For Your Personal Growth.

The Role of Culture. Living in a Combat Zone. The Rituals of Life. Following Our Leaders. Learning Through Intimidation. Worshiping the Root of Evil. Selling Us Out. Our Religious Heritage. Our Genetic Heritage. The Ways We Grow. Love is a Many-Splintered Thing. Learned Incompetence. Following Family Traditions. When Daddy's an Addict. Family Genetics. The Outcome. For Your Personal Growth.

Do You Know the Way to San Diego? Our Maps Versus the Territory. The Natural Lie. Organic Versus Machinelike Man. The Self as Universe. Core Beliefs of Addiction. Going the Wrong Way. Going the Right Way. "The Void" and "The Nova." Powerlessness Over Addictions. The Myth of Self-Control. For Your Personal Growth.

## Advanced Recovery

A Sense of Coherence. Honesty. Unconditional Loving. Fear of Love. Competence. For Your Personal Growth.

## Putting It All Together

Recovery Core Beliefs. Positive Social Supports and Ties. Committed Relationships. Ability to Maintain Loving Relationships. Committed Spirituality. Rational, Flexible, and Farsighted Strategy. Material Stability. Adequate Intelligence and Knowledge. Genetic Makeup. Persistence.

# ACKNOWLEDGMENTS

My thanks to all the people who contributed to this book. The therapists, clients, and friends who gave ideas, criticism, and time made such improvements in the final draft, that this is as much their book as mine.

Special thanks to Kathy and Maggie, the two who were most willing to help and cater to my artistic self-centeredness for two years. I can't thank you enough.

Additional thanks to the owners and staff of Westside Guidance Center for their support, for allowing me to take up so much computer time and space, and for the financial support to finish the project. Also, I acknowledge the invaluable editorial contribution of Pat Holliday.

A final thanks to my other friends and family who believed I could write when I wondered.

# FOREWORD

We are taught at very early ages that depression and pain are abnormal. We are taught "place two in the mouth, son." Pharmaceutical companies even named medicines after saints - St. Joseph's aspirin.

In the last one hundred years we have moved from a society that comes together to produce, to a society that comes together to consume. As consumers, most of us are judged by our toys, degrees, drugs, and occupations. America, in so many ways, is an externally oriented, consuming and addictive society. Power and addiction are American legacies.

In *Rational Madness: The Paradox of Addiction*, Ray Hoskins expands our understanding of addiction. He eloquently combines alcohol/drug addiction theory, family system theory, the self-medication hypothesis, addictive life styles research and other schools of thought into a unifying concept. *Rational Madness* defines addiction as part of a life-long central coping style typically accompanied by other addictions. For clinicians who have worked with chemical and other addictions, this should be particularly confirming. How often have we treated alcoholism and discovered the untreated and surrogate addictions to food, gambling and sex?

Of great important to the future of our country is the interruption and prevention of the familial aspects of addictive life styles. For those in recovery or families trying to understand and/or cope with addiction this book can be a valuable asset. For those professionals, in all disciplines, who treat addiction, the book can broaden understanding. Ray Hoskins has written a gift.

October, 1988                                         Cardwell C. Nuckols

# PROLOGUE

In the summer of 1979, I gave a talk on healthy coping styles for a group of addictions workers in western Michigan. After the presentation, a member of the audience came up to me and shared that she was an editor for a university publishing house, and that I should publish my material. For the first time, I seriously considered doing so, although the thought had occurred to me earlier in the year.

"I am not awake" began a journal entry that previous February. While dealing with a divorce and being a part-time parent, I realized that my self-involvement prevented me from seeing my circumstances and surroundings clearly. Mired in grief, pain, and fear, I couldn't appreciate anything but those feelings. It was impossible to feel otherwise. Part of my mind wasn't operating. It was partially asleep.

My marriage, which had recently ended, was based on fear and insecurity, not love. The ending grief was just the period on the sentence we had written for ourselves. The fear had limited our coping options and we failed because we didn't know how to keep it alive.

Following this realization of my handicaps in sustaining relationships, I decided to develop new intimacy skills. Since then, there have been several unforeseen results which led me to write this book.

Like most of us, I learned relationship patterns in my family. During my childhood there was a good deal of stress and periodic abuse in the family. Most of the abuse focused on my mother and me. Even though my father's emotional outbursts were related to medication for his chronic asthma, I didn't understand this and spent much of the time afraid and confused. My mother, sisters, and brother shared these feelings.

As the family operated in fear, this fear pervaded our strategies for emotional survival both within the family and within the society. Looking back, this environment was much like that of an alcoholic family and we had many of the traits of such families.

My mother, father, and I were in a rescuer, persecutor, and victim role-play in which dad remained the persecutor. Mom and I switched back and forth between the roles of victim and rescuer. Later, dad shared the ways in which he felt persecuted too. We all believed we were victims.

This background led me to be most comfortable in situations wherein my primary role was rescuing or caretaking of others. When the chance came to be an addictions counselor, it sounded ideal.

Like most members of chaotic families who become therapists, I had several years of burnout and tension because of approaching the work as a caretaker. The constant danger of client failure triggered my insecurities and I became uncomfortable. I paid a penalty in exhaustion and depression. This also created negative effects in my relationships.

Since I had spent the previous years dealing with several different populations of addicts, by 1979 some of the commonalities between different addictions were unmistakable. My search had begun for more answers. There had to be larger patterns.

Soon, I discovered the works of two writers, Lawrence Hatterer, M.D., and Kenneth Keyes. Two very different people, they presented two distinct, but complementary views of addiction. Hatterer, in *The Pleasure Addicts*, stated that an underlying "addictive process" was present in all addiction. He made the point that the specific addiction was less important than the addictive "coping style" itself. He listed several addictions I had never considered as such.

Ken Keyes, in his *Handbook To Higher Consciousness*, claimed that addictions were "emotion-backed demands for security, sensations, and power." My own work and my life soon verified his ideas.

When I read these books, I became quite frustrated because they offered strong evidence of both work and food addictions in my life. These weren't complete surprises, but the books allowed me to face the addictions with more honesty. Just like my clients, I had addictions.

It later became obvious that there were three addictions in my life: work, relationships, and food. These addictive options had always been there. As in every addiction, there had been denial. Plus, the denial mechanisms for the three addictions had supported each other. I would cope with the problems caused by one addiction by using the other two to treat my feelings. Challenging any one of the addictions resulted in urges to balance by increasing the urgency of the others.

This pattern of addictions seemed to be some form of stable "complex." It had developed over several years as I had focused on those fixes which seemed to work best for me. The study of these complexes in myself and others contributed to the model presented here. It also led me to a happier life. The recovery from my own addictions continues and my life is no longer centered on just three major sources of meaning. This book is, in part, a celebration of these changes.

There are several case examples presented in this book, and it is possible that you will recognize yourself or someone you know in the descriptions. Many of my clients will see parts of themselves. This is more because we are so much alike than it is because we are so unique. While the facts in these cases are true, the clients themselves and the facts are blends of several people I have known. None of my individual clients are here as case examples. If I were to use individual clients, it would compromise their confidentiality, which is wrong.

In another clarification, unless data is specifically relevant to women, I have used the male pronoun as a means of making the volume more readable. I have mixed feelings about this, but my editor convinced me that this is the only reasonable solution in a volume so large. I apologize in advance to any of my female readers who might take offense at this style.

After years of effort, the goal is finally achieved. I offer this volume to you in hopes that it will shorten your search for answers to your personal questions about addiction and add to the quality and meaning in your life. If it does so, I will consider *Rational Madness* a success.

# INTRODUCTION

*What we live with, we learn . . .*
*What we learn, we practice . . .*
*What we practice, we become.*
                              - Earnie Larsen

It's everywhere! From the performers who enter well-known treatment centers for "exhaustion," to the sports figures forced into treatment for drug addiction, to the television specials on bulimia and molested children, addiction is hot and examined every day in the media. Yet, when most of us think of addiction we think of one addiction, such as alcoholism or drug addiction. It is difficult to describe and understand all addiction.

## Gaining Perspective

There is much debate on the definition of addiction. Some scientists, for example, consider compulsive overeating an addiction, while others do not. The same argument surrounds bulimia, anorexia, sexual compulsiveness, and other commonly treated problems. I see this dispute arising not so much out of the facts of addiction, as out of the limited views of those who are trying to make sense of this crazy behavior.

Most of us who are absorbed in this topic are either addicts in recovery from chemical problems, persons who have other addictions, or adult children of persons suffering from addictions or other neurotic problems. Others are scientists with their own categories to protect, and their own ways of viewing reality which reflect their own specialties. This has limited the evolution of our knowledge, and created some confusion about addiction similar to that of the confusion of the blind men in the Hindu fable of the blind men and the elephant.

In this fable, some blind men were asked to describe an elephant. One of them touched the elephant's tail and decided that the elephant was much like a rope. Another felt his trunk and decided that it was much like a snake. Still another touched his leg and concluded that the others were wrong, because the elephant was really like a tree. This was very puzzling to the man who was feeling the elephant's leaf-like ear. The lack of an ability to see the whole was resulting in confusing interpretations of the meaning of the parts.

This document describes the whole elephant, with little focus on the parts. This is much like stepping back to see new angles on any scene in photography. When our viewpoint shifts on any object, the object does not change. It only seems to. We simply see more or different details than from other angles. This can also occur in considering addiction as a general phenomenon, rather than just focusing on alcoholism, co-dependency, or any other single addiction.

If we continue the fable metaphor, then addictive process is the whole, or the elephant. Alcoholism could be the front right leg, with cocaine addiction being its tail. Sex addiction might be the elephant's ear. Just as the blind men were not able to perceive the whole elephant, and made faulty assumptions, the alcoholism expert will tend to make false assumptions about the sex or food addict. We need to step back and develop a view of the whole, of all addictions in combination, in order to make meaningful jumps in knowledge. Let us begin by considering one person's life in which there were several problem addictions.

**Stalking The Perfect Orgasm**

Karen was a sex addict. At least this was the reason she came to see me. Steve, her husband, had seen me earlier about a drug problem and had asked her to attend counseling because of the breakdown of their marriage. He believed that she had left him because of his drug use.

Karen presented a very different outlook on her decision. Although Steve's drug use had been a problem, she had really left because her sex life had become so dominant that she couldn't hide it from him much longer. She was having sexual meetings with two or three men a day during the week and with four or more men per day during weekends. She was guilt-ridden, afraid of disease, and felt totally unworthy of her husband or any other man.

As the picture unfolded, it was obvious that Steve had known of her strong sex drive and had encouraged it in the early years of their relationship. They had tried swinging for a while, but she had quit because she always wanted more and feared he wouldn't be able to accept her hidden desires to have several men at once and to try homosexuality. They had also used drugs together on weekends. She had had isolated sexual flings during the course of the marriage, but the reckless pattern she described to me began two years earlier when she entered a very high pressure sales firm.

The atmosphere within this firm was very work-addictive. The employees were to put the needs of the company above personal and family needs. Karen's secretary/receptionist position put her in contact with many men and she found their attention exciting. As these men talked, she was offered sex constantly. Slowly, she started having sexual flings with some of them.

Finally, her bosses became aware of her behavior and approached her. When she entered treatment, she was having sex with both of her supervisors and neither of them knew she was seeing the other. Both were married. The picture that evolved was complicated. Karen had always been sexually wild. She and Steve had experimented with sex and drugs within their marriage. Finally, Steve lost control of his drug use and she lost control of her sex habit.

The beginning of both problems happened years before when Steve drank with his alcoholic father and when Karen's minister-father molested her. In both cases, these early experiences had been very intense, but not pleasureful. Karen had always lacked attention from her father, but one incident in which they mastur-bated each other stood out in her mind. During her father's orgasm was the first time she had ever had any feelings of power or control over him. This ability to control men's bodily reactions became the essence of her sexuality. She could only be orgasmic with her husband. It was this power over her partners which she sought in her addiction, not the sensations of sex.

Karen and Steve each had work-addictive families and each developed a work-addictive problem which delayed their having children. They also had a roller-coaster relationship. He shared her sex addiction through swinging and she shared his drug addiction by using with him. They had often fought about the problems the addictions caused, but each believed everything would be fine if the other would change.

With treatment and self-help, both Karen and Steve recovered. Neither has had outside sexual affairs and both of them have been drug-free for the three years. Their relationship has improved; she has stopped both overworking and ignoring her own and her family's needs. It has been a hard three years, but both of them consider this the best time of their lives.

Karen's case, and that of her husband Steve, shows the problems often present in dealing with addiction. As new addic-tions are discovered and named, we begin to understand the connections between persons with addictions and their choosing which addictions to practice in their attempts to cope with reality. It appears that all addictions result from the same basic coping pattern.

Hatterer, in *The Pleasure Addicts*, argued that addiction was a pattern of reacting to small amounts of pain by reaching for all the pleasure we can get. Much like a hunter, the addict "stalks" the perfect orgasm, high, job, person, or other object which is believed to cause pleasure.

**Coping With The Symptoms**

I first began to understand addictive coping in the early 1970's, when working with Dr. H. Stephen Glenn, a leader in alcohol and drug abuse prevention. At that time, the national campaigns about drug abuse stated that drug abuse was not the problem, it was the symptom. As he explored this idea, Dr. Glenn saw that drug abuse was not the symptom, or the initial problem, but rather it was a treatment for symptoms of problems. Furthermore, it had no hope of solving anything, because problems were ignored when the emotional state was the true focus of self-treatment.

Successful coping has a response aimed at the actual problem, while addictive coping attacks the symptoms (feelings) with potentially dire consequences. Another way of saying this is that the addictive coping choice is to cope with oneself, rather than to cope with external reality. This is a closed, circular style of coping, which ignores actual problems.

### Successful Coping

| Problem | Symptom | Response (treatment) |
|---|---|---|
| *strep throat* | *pain* | *anxiety* |
| *bad marriage* | *anxiety* | *marriage counseling* |
| *peer pressure to use drugs* | *anxiety* | *say "NO," and leave* |

### Addictive Coping

| Problem | Symptom | Response (treatment) |
|---|---|---|
| *strep throat* | *pain* | *aspirin* |
| *bad marriage* | *anxiety* | *Valium* |
| *peer pressure* | *anxiety* | *give in to use drugs* |

In this example, the first person's addictive coping risks a severe infection, while the second person risks a Valium addiction. In some cases, the short-term use of aspirin for the pain of infection is wise, but not when antibiotics are needed to kill the infection. Similarly, Valium is sometimes useful for anxiety symptom control while receiving counseling, but it should not be used without a treatment plan focused on actual problems. In both situations, the focus of responses on the problem itself offers obvious benefits. In the third example, the person asked to use drugs has an option to comply with his friend's requests to feel accepted, or say "No" and leave. If he gives in to fear of scorn, he risks developing chemical dependency later.

Imagine yourself at a friend's house and the friend is sitting with you in the living room and complaining that his house plants are dying from lack of water. All the while he complains, he eats from a large bowl of chocolate-covered raisins. He is already overweight. You know there is a sink in the kitchen and you have even seen a pitcher for watering house plants. Yet your friend is just sitting eating candy and complaining, rather than solving his problem.

Addictive coping follows the above pattern. It always focuses on self-medicating feelings, rather than on solving problems. When you look closely at it, it is always just as crazy as the behavior in the preceding example. Yet, for some reason, it is widespread.

Addiction is a false path to meaning, based on false beliefs, inept coping behaviors, and a basic self-centeredness which treats symptoms instead of coping with reality. This symptom-treating behavior is so natural in our culture that it is very difficult to see, much less change. When this symptom-treating model becomes a major part of a person's life, he is in an addictive process, a process in which he regularly uses addictive behavior to cope with internal and external problems. When the behaviors become habitual, the person has one or more addictions. If he continues, the process will reach its endpoint of addictive "disease."

**What Is Addictive Process?**

Addictive Process is a coping style in which a person habitually responds to reality by using fix-oriented behaviors to produce desired feelings rather than by responding directly to the immediate demands in his life. This process may include several or only a few addictive behaviors or addictions. Both the types of addictive options which people use and the thought processes which underlie such a coping method are explored here. *Rational Madness* also describes in detail just how this process works.

**Security, Sensation, and Power**

One of the major issues is understanding the emotional purposes of addictive behavior. The desired feelings produced by addictive behavior fall into three broad types: feelings of security, physical sensations, and feelings of power or control over oneself or others. Karen's sex addiction had all three types of feelings, but her primary fix is one of power over others. The addict tries to replace uncomfortable feelings with as much security, sensation, and power feelings as possible. These feelings seem to operate on a continuum, with security fixes being somewhat damaging, sensation fixes more damaging, and power fixes most damaging. Getting an alcohol "buzz" is a sensation fix. Getting drunk is gaining total control over one's feelings. Many people drink to get high and have few problems. Those who always drink to get drunk have many problems. This pattern holds true, no matter what addiction is explored. This issue is reviewed throughout the book.

The book's title of *Rational Madness* describes the thought processes of the addict as he defends the addiction(s) practiced. Addictive behavior will always look insane to an outsider, but it seems wholly rational to the person engaged in the behavior. There is a logic to addictive behavior, but that logic is based on unrealistic fear, a childlike manner of viewing the world, and faulty, but unchallenged, premises.

The major themes of addiction presented here are:

1. **Addictive coping patterns** are ingrained in most cultures to the extent that people use them thoughout their lives. In sociological terms, it is therefore "normal" behavior. So while most addictions lead to abnormal behavior, they evolve out of beliefs and behaviors ingrained in society. The learning process underlying these patterns exists at a societal level and filters down through all institutions, including the basic societal unit, the family.

2. **For each individual,** addiction reflects problems within his mental model or map of reality. This map is based upon false core beliefs and upon a highly self-centered view of reality. This produces much fear and many empty feelings. The addiction becomes a method of self-control used to treat the fear arising from having this faulty model.

3. **A major distortion** in an addict's belief system is in his beliefs about relationships. The primary confusion occurs in the addict's relationship with himself, and this is projected outward, causing problems in his relationships with others. These relationships themselves then become addictive.

4. **There are several other addictions** which we develop. Some of these addictions are considered bad, but some are encouraged by the society. Some are to substances, and others are to behavioral processes. All cause damage when practiced to extreme. Each has its own characteristics and problems.

5. **Each addiction is part** of a comprehensive coping style which I describe as addictive process. There are five stages in this process, beginning with innocent enhancement behaviors, and ending with addictive disease which can be fatal.

6. **This addictive process is progressive,** no matter what combinations of addictions may occur. As the addictions progress, the purposes for behavior evolve from security fixes to sensation fixes to power fixes. The process will become more and more disruptive to a person's life unless the whole process, not just one addiction, is arrested.

**7. Addictions become focused in complexes** in which each addiction reinforces the others. The more addictions in a person's complex, the more comfortable he will be. Persons usually try to recover once they can no longer maintain three or more addictive options in their lives.

**8. There are predictable patterns** in the relationships between one individual's addictions and the addictions of those closest to him. These patterns occur in family groups and continue, generation after generation. The patterns transfer both genetically and socially across generations and combine to make children of addicts high-risk candidates to develop the addictions of their families and other addictions.

**9. Addictive behavior is based on fearful feelings** and is a normal part of the learning process for us all in our psychological development. When it becomes a coping style, however, it serves to retard normal maturation and produce an emotionally retarded person. It slows the process of emotional growth to such a degree that addictive people in middle age will often show emotional patterns of adolescence.

**10. Maturation is analogous to recovery.** Recovery from addictions consists of continuing in the process of maturation which was slowed down by the addictions. Beginning recovery needs to occur in group settings so that the addict can finish the peer-focused stage of adolescence and finish developing his individual identity. The more emotional maturity the addict develops, the more stable his recovery.

**11. There are established patterns of successful change** which addicts use in recovery. Addicts can follow these patterns for best results.

**12. Since addiction reflects distorted models of reality,** the recovering person needs to develop both new models of reality and new coping strategies to be successful. He will need to learn these strategies from others and from study. If he does so, there is much hope.

The subject matter of this book is quite broad. This is to attain the goal of presenting a complete model. The intent of this effort is to develop better insight into the organizing aspects of addiction. Though the scope of the book is quite sweeping, addiction is just one of several ways someone's model of the world limits his perceived options for coping. As Bandler and Grinder have mentioned, "In most, if not all, mental-emotional dysfunction, the limitation is not in the world. The limitation exists primarily in the person's beliefs about the world." In addiction, the addict's beliefs about the world are limited, and this creates a great amount of pain as he pursues pleasure.

You are invited to join in this effort to expand the view and treatment of addictions. If you find yourself angry, frustrated, or having other strong feelings as a result of reading this book, keep reading. You may be discovering addictions of your own.

### For Your Personal Growth

*Look at your life and try to identify areas in which you often attempt to cope with problems by treating your feelings while the problems get worse.*

*Now think of some alternatives which may offer better outcomes. The next time you face one of these problems, try one of the alternatives you have identified.*

# ADDICTION IN SOCIETY

*If we love this society in which we live, we must be willing to confront the reality that it has a disease. Like an alcoholic, it is not bad and trying to get good. It is sick and trying to get well.*
                                                    - Anne Wilson-Schaef

**The** President and his wife go on television to announce a major new offensive against drug abuse. A researcher in San Francisco finds that eighty-five percent of eighteen-year-old girls in her study were dieters and all had shown behaviors connected with eating disorders. A report surfaces about college girls going out, bingeing on food, and returning home and purging the food in a bulimic episode. A national outcry is developing about the dangers of the newest dangerous, cheap drug, "crack." These stories are recent, and are part of the pattern of addictive coping in America.

The seeds of addiction are in us all. Addictive beliefs and coping patterns are so ingrained in Western cultures that most people follow them throughout their lives. Therefore, they seem to be normal patterns when followed in moderation.

We all behave, at times, in ways which could lead to addictions under the right circumstances. Most of us have found ourselves either too dependent on a relationship, or defining who we are by our job, or having a drink because we felt we needed one. We feel a rush of excitement at anticipating our favorite "fixes." Between our urges for alcohol, food, sex, things, work, or reassurance from a loved one, few of us get through most days without experiencing a desire for a fix. The more intense our urges, the more likely we are to be coping in ways that make us unhappy.

Given that we all engage in addictive behaviors to some extent, the issue becomes one of understanding why some of us become involved in addictions that are very destructive to our lives, while others are more mildly affected. The first part of the issue is simple. It is easy to explain why people become addicted. It is much more difficult to explain how some of us avoid this fate.

## The Role of Culture

All the forces discussed in this chapter create a framework we call culture. We are citizens of a world, countries, communities, and families which establish the norms, or guidelines, within which we all live. A culture serves to give us easy, workable guidelines for our conduct. What we wear, how and what we eat, our method and frequency of bathing and other such behaviors are culturally sanctioned. *All societies and cultures have both healthy and unhealthy aspects*. Our culture is fix-oriented. A fix-oriented culture teaches its members to obtain happiness and meaning by pursuing external objects. This creates difficulties.

Aaron Antonovsky, in *Health, Stress, and Coping*, states that a stable culture is a prime "resistance resource" to stress. Culture gives us "magic" answers to complex situations, answers below the level of our analytic awareness, which are the foundation of our coping philosophy. He also states that we can consider the lack of a stable culture a stressor for its members. The culture provides the stability in our maps of reality and the family derives most of its beliefs from the culture. When the cultural map is flawed, so are our lives.

In Western culture, indeed in our world, we are in the midst of the most rapid change processes in the history of man. Yet, we have not changed our organic reality. In spite of this, our present view of mankind is mechanistic. To paraphrase Herb Goldberg, the ideal American male is a machine. Due to the changes in women's roles, we all face pressure to be "productive individuals" throughout our life-cycles. Yet we still experience the organic changes which have been occurring at certain times in life ever since mankind has existed. Even our medical approach is to fix broken parts and restore the patient's functioning.

The "magic" answers to which Antonovsky refers have broken down. We have lost many of the key cultural rituals which once helped us cope. In their place, we have learned to plug different "fixes" into ourselves in vain attempts to produce meaning and happiness. In place of rites of passage, prayer, discussion, and vision quests, we have shopping, casual sex, drinking, working, falling in love, and several other addictive processes. How much have we lost in the trade?

Ideal cultures do not exist. At best, a culture provides a trade-off in the competition between individual and group needs. Ideally, a culture should give the most mental, physical, and emotional health to those persons who most closely follow its norms. In our culture, when we follow the norms, we risk developing dominant addictions. For example, seventy to eighty percent of the adult population of our culture drinks alcohol. We know that a certain percentage of the drinking population will develop a harmful, even fatal, addiction to alcohol. Yet it remains "normal" to drink.

We now know that a major ingredient in whether one becomes alcoholic is a genetic predisposition. A person develops alcoholism by participating in normal behavior which triggers this genetic flaw. He loses control before he recognizes a developing problem. The cultural norms lead into a genetic trap of which he is unaware.

In much the same way, it now appears that persons with overeating problems have biochemical factors which predispose them to being overweight. Our culture has historically taught us to eat high fat, high calorie foods for enjoyment. Some people can't successfully survive on our national diet without becoming obese or developing cardiovascular disease.

Addictive beliefs are not the only beliefs being taught in Western societies, but they are taught as options. This makes it inevitable that some people will adopt these beliefs as methods of achieving meaning and happiness. Let's explore our cultural confusion.

## Living In A Combat Zone

In spite of our society's affluence and power, we have a societal view that we live in a hostile world and need to rely on military and economic power to survive. Accordingly, many of us develop tenacious fears of the external world and of each other. We calculate our strategies for surviving and succeeding in this "cold, cruel world." We use fear as a guide to survival throughout our lives. Such fear becomes a constant stressor, and prevents individual serenity.

Any constant stressor makes it very difficult for us to feel comfortable and creates frequent anxiety. When we approach life from a fearful stance, it becomes difficult to distinguish between real and illusory threats. In this mindset, we can see a threat in almost everything. That can be overwhelming.

The trend is to search for some external "fix" to treat all anxiety. Using the addictive behavior model outlined previously, treating symptoms seems the most reasonable choice, since it doesn't appear to most of us that we can cure the anxiety itself.

Many of us constantly worry about our survival. It is common to see persons whose income is more than one hundred thousand dollars a year worried about financial survival. Other people convince themselves that the breakup of a love relationship threatens their total survival. There are other patterns which show this inability to tell real from illusory threats.

An approach to fear which consists of treating emotions, instead of confronting problems, magnifies our desires for outside stimulation. Whether we have been sexually attracted to someone, felt we needed an alcoholic beverage, craved a hot fudge sundae, wanted a new car, or felt we had to be more financially successful in order to feel worthwhile, the experience of wanting a "fix" is common to us all.

This *external orientation* to sex, the right clothes, right friends, material items, or ice cream is so ingrained in our societal beliefs that most of us respond automatically when we see an object of our desire. We all feel pleasure from having our desires met, and we use this to relieve boredom. This value of stimulation is a major part of our cultural beliefs and is becoming more so daily. We find objects outside of ourselves to create happiness.

## The Rituals Of Life

Addictive behaviors are taught in many social rituals. While a common view is that addiction begins when we use addictive behavior to reduce pain, this is incorrect. We usually view rituals as pleasure-giving experiences, yet addiction begins there. The twenty-year-old looks forward to his next birthday and the time in the bars with his friends. We drink at parties, and many use other chemicals. Courtship rituals focus almost totally on sexual attractiveness and financial status. These rituals will not provide us with lasting love. There are birthday parties, holiday banquets, shopping sprees, eating contests, drinking contests, even bingeing and purging contests among college coeds. There are swingers' groups, bachelor parties, and Sunday afternoon football cheerleaders. There are materialism-based social movements, status credit cards, and religious leaders who expect "true believers" to send them checks in the mail.

If the early experiences with a behavior aren't positive, that behavior will not bring pleasure later in life. We all learn to attach a positive value to an addictive behavior before we use it to treat pain. The process of switching from pleasure-seeking to pain-treating may take very little time, but one must establish the belief that a behavior will make him feel better before he will use it for self-treatment. The varied rituals in which we stress addictive behavior help us learn this option.

## Following Our Leaders

Our role models, with their addictions to alcohol, drugs, sex, power, relationships, and food, reinforce our own addiction, too. Some recover and become public examples of the recovery path for the rest of us. More of our celebrities are stating that addiction is not an acceptable way to fit in or feel good. Unfortunately, there are fewer examples of those who recover than reports of the dramatic problems of our athletes, actors, politicians, and others.

The most effective form of teaching occurs when the student identifies with the teacher. Then the student will follow the example set for him. When we discover that people we admire are addicts, it reduces our resistance to addiction.

## Learning Through Intimidation

Our educational institutions teach us how to gain the skills we need to pursue the society's materialistic model of success and they discourage behavior which is spontaneous, loving, and brilliant. We are taught to rank competition and power over cooperation and loving behaviors. We are expected to accept hypocrisy and incompetence in institutions, while being taught to "think for ourselves." They say to "say no" to drugs and premarital sex, but to "say yes" to the pursuit of material happiness.

Also, we're taught to enjoy competing with, and achieving mastery over, our fellow human beings in sports and family relationships. We receive a double message here. Winning, or showing mastery (power), enhances the meaning of the competition and losing reduces the meaning. Our feeling good becomes dependent, therefore, on our winning. But few can always win.

This develops family, school, and playground hierarchies in which we feel good if we are leaders, and depressed if we go unnoticed. This competition for control in social situations teaches us to see others as objects to manipulate in a search for power. This level of addiction is potentially the most harmful of all.

Furthermore, society expects us to become individuals during our teens and early adulthood in institutions which discourage individuality. At times, especially for gifted students, it seems that educational institutions are structured to inhibit the very traits which allow students to be most creative and productive. We normally outgrow the complying, simply adaptive, level of development by fourteen, but remain in institutions which expect it of us far beyond that age.

**Worshiping The Root Of Evil**

The whole economic structure of our society is based on our remaining good materialists. This is unlikely to change. We have progressed economically to where both men and women are equally able to strive to be happy by purchasing thousands of large and small trinkets, while keeping so busy they have no time for each other. Some of us worship BMWs, Porsches, Mercedes, and other expensive cars. We want large houses with ecstacy-providing hot tubs and up-to-date kitchen appliances. We must change our basic personalities so that we can have better "career paths." All the while, our economy is becoming less productive and competitive as more of us react negatively to being treated like machines, and many of us turn to chemicals in the workplace. The net effect of this direction in society is to mislead us in our life's quest to believe that these objects of societal desire and paths of achievement for achievement's sake will provide meaning, love, identity, and happiness in our lives.

**Selling Us Out**

Advertising often takes advantage of our fearful perceptions. The advertiser creates perceptions of threat, then presents a "product" which will insure our well-being. Once we accept the threat, we shift into a level of survival consciousness, and we believe the rational thing to do is purchase the product.

Advertisers nurture certain addictions with massive advertising campaigns. One must create the myth of needing a new fix before people will choose the particular new fix offered by the advertiser. For example, we sit around at night and see that it is "Miller Time," and that "the night belongs to Michelob." We see shots of "the best beer bellies in America," which look suspiciously like genital areas, alternating with pictures of beer cans. We watch Saturday morning cartoons and see how healthy the cereals are which have their sugar fortified with vitamins A, C, and D. Our adult advertising implies that almost anything we buy will result in sex with people who look like Greek gods and goddesses. The good life in the movies has plenty of food, drink, drugs, and sex, not to mention money.

This list could go on forever, for the fix list in our culture is ever expanding. Yet, no one has ever achieved happiness in such a surface manner. We all know this at some level, but we still partially believe the advertising myths. As a result, many in our society know that the way to be happy is to have an intense and highly sexual relationship with an attractive person, to get rich, to have all the "in" things, to take "Miller Time," to win at the track, to eat in the best restaurants, to have a large house and a maid, to have political power, to be married, to travel . . .

## Our Religious Heritage

I often watch the environmental shows on public television. These reveal how Western culture differs from some Eastern ones in its religious beliefs and how those differences affect the environment. Western man sees himself above nature, while Eastern man sees himself as a part of it. This produces drastically different environmental values. We are seldom taught respect for the environment in our culture.

Our religious values support addiction as our culture prepares us to damage our environment. Our religious leaders teach a strong belief in self-control and avoidance of sin. Our theology often teaches fear of God and induces guilt, convinced that this will help us be better persons. We receive little similar indoctrination on respecting the balance of both our internal and external environments as a means of survival. The values we teach are too often organizational values instead of higher spiritual values. We experience an inherent tendency to perfectionism and judgmentalism in much of our religious tradition. All this supports the addictive mythology.

## Our Genetic Heritage

Recent research has shown genetic patterns in addictions to alcohol, cocaine, and food. It is known that the genetic pool of a culture will have some effect upon its characteristics. This effect is difficult to precisely measure. Because of this, there are those who resist admitting any genetic influence at all in addiction. For my part, the evidence of genetic components of addiction is too overwhelming to ignore. For example, we know that Irish Catholics seem to have a high rate of alcoholism while Italian Catholics do not. There seems to be more susceptibility to certain addictions depending upon your ancestry. The most dramatic evidence in our society seems to be the effect of alcohol on descendants of the American Indian population.

## The Ways We Grow

Erikson, Maslow, Kohlberg, Sheehy, Hall, and others have written about human development stages. They are all in substantial agreement about the contents of the stages, even though they offer minor differences of opinion about the timing and details of these stages. The pace at which we develop seems to be influenced by the norms within the society we inhabit. Developmental process is affected by the opportunities a society provides for its members to learn more mature adaptive patterns. The dominance of addictive coping within our culture inhibits our ability to mature.

In another sense, however, the limits on a person's growth arise from the perceptions of that unique individual. We all have our beliefs, our "models" of how the world works and of our place in it. It is in these models that the problem begins. The critical phase for those interested in understanding addiction seems to be the largely adolescent stage of developing a sense of independent identity. We all experience stages in our human development, before adolescence and during the first few years of that period, in which we focus almost totally on the bodily or physical level of experience. At that time, it was difficult to distinguish short-term pleasure from long-term happiness.

Most of us begin our experimentation with the major societal addictions during these adolescent and pre-adolescent years. We are, for biological reasons, more centered on our bodies and the sensations of our bodies during adolescence than at later stages of development. For this reason, early experiences with chemicals, sex, thrills, and relationships produce very intense feelings. I have found that these early experiences are the ones addicted people remember most fondly when they recall their histories.

The increasing length of functional adolescence in our society is an important aspect of addiction today. My college sociology classes discussed the effects of an extended period of adolescence. This stage is only significant in industrialized countries and has very little place in the organic processes of psychological development.

The American economy has changed drastically in the last twenty years. It is very difficult to get out of high school and become a productive, self-supporting member of society. Young people are spending longer and longer periods of time financially dependent on their families. This, in and of itself, creates a developmental crisis for the young person, not to mention the parents. Adolescence is a period in which the only significant role we play in society is becoming educated. After that, we need to get on with the process of individuation. Our society is not dealing with this issue.

Today's adolescents receive much peer pressure to participate in addictive behaviors. Industrialized societies intensify the addictive pleasure-seeking learned during the developmental stage of adolescence and those closest to the adolescent further reinforce it. Most of us learned to drink, make friends, and be sexual during this period of our lives. It is easy to mistake for true happiness the intensity of pleasure experienced during this time and to spend our lives trying to recapture those feelings, instead of proceeding with the maturation process and learning to have the real thing. So, adolescents are in a race to outgrow the addictive behaviors before they become addictions.

In the addictions treatment field, we recognize that some people become so caught up in a search for adolescent intensity that they remain emotional adolescents at whatever age they enter treatment. For these persons, we consider our task one of habilitation, or bringing someone to normal levels of functioning for the first time, rather than rehabilitation, or returning someone to a pre-existing level of competence.

There are other times in our lives in which addiction often develops around developmental issues. Two major times are following a major loss, such as in divorce or the death of a loved one, and following retirement. When people use fixes to treat the pain of major transitions, they risk developing an addiction.

## Love Is A Many-Splintered Thing

Our models of love and marriage are also addictive and create much harm. We have many cultural myths of "romantic love" which lead us to believe in the fairy tale that we can fall in love with someone who is our opposite and successfully live with him or her the rest of our lives. In the last thirty years, this myth has become more complicated as our divorce rate has skyrocketed. It is hard to live with someone who has nothing in common with you except a short period of exciting, romantic love.

## Learned Incompetence

So our cultural norms for sex, work, materialism, risk-taking, and relationships provide faulty models for coping. We are, however, mostly unaware of this cultural flaw and use these addictive models. When we do so, we become less competent at actual tension management, because addictive coping fails to address the causes of our tension.

Culturally approved behaviors are overtaught with painful consequences. In another example, eating is positive behavior. It is necessary for survival, yet we ostracize the person who over-learns the positive value of eating and becomes obese. Relationships between the sexes are necessary to the culture's survival, yet we avoid persons who become too dependent within relationships and who talk about them incessantly. The ground rules seem to be to participate in addictive coping in moderation and we will accept you, too much, and we won't.

For the person who needs treatment for addiction, this ground rule doesn't work. In the addictive client, there may be moderation within the use of a particular addictive behavior, but there is little or no variation in his or her preference for coping by seeking a fix. Upon entering treatment, it is obvious to almost everyone that the style is not working.

Many of us who have never felt a need for treatment feel the emotional and physical "hangovers" from our food, work, material, relationship, and other addictive behaviors, but we do not yet recognize that we are dealing with potential addictions. The culture is in flux even around addiction and recovery. We are seeing acceptability evolving for those who have defeated one of several addictions. Adult children of alcoholics are organizing and holding meetings, and we are seeing a new "anonymous" self help group every few months. This may be a groundswell reaction to our instinctive need to force new rituals into our current culture. I hope so. These rituals are badly needed.

## Following Family Traditions

As stated earlier, almost all behaviors which lead to addiction have positive value in their original context. We learn to be fix-oriented in situations which often seem the most positive of our young lives. In spite of our feelings that addiction evolves out of "peer pressure," most of our addictive training occurs within our families.

The family is the most important single institution in our quest to make sense of the universe. We have family histories, traditions, and beliefs which do much to shape our perception of the world. Even within the closed and small family structure, the perceptions of family members vary widely. Still, there will be many similarities between the models of reality held by members of the same family. All our families are part of the culture, and will reflect that culture. We will be alternately supported and buffeted by the cultural winds of the society. There are, however, opportunities in almost any family to perceive addictive coping as a viable option.

For example, most of our families have rituals in which food is an integral part of close family activities. In our homes, we reward children with food, making eating, love, and security synonymous in the mind of the child. By doing so, we help the child build a more intense emotional demand for food than is necessary for appropriate eating. At family gatherings we enhance the warm, intimate feelings by having a feast. The child is taught to eat more for the sensation of eating and the security of being with people than for nutrition. We can observe this in ourselves at family gatherings, when we feel an intense urge to get on with the meal. These reward systems are linked with overeating in adult life.

These "enhancement" experiences can be both general and specific in form. The alcoholism literature has long reflected that families in isolated subcultures have lower rates of addiction to alcohol because the enhancement experiences with alcohol operate in very specific settings. This is combined with very strong rules against use of alcohol outside of those settings. In these groups, intoxication is strongly discouraged. This specific use of enhancement experiences with alcohol seems to create little damage. On the other hand, families who use alcohol liberally to celebrate anything have excessive alcoholism. These general patterns of enhancing experience with alcohol, or other potentially addictive chemicals or behavior, seem to lead to the generalized coping style of addiction.

The more we use addictive coping options in a family, the more likely we are to develop an addictive style. In another example, there are families in which children only receive attention from their parents in response to working. Some families even have most of the parent-child closeness structured within working contexts. All the "important" things the family does are work-related. The message is that work and intimacy are synonymous. This teaches the child that getting his emotional needs met will require work. This makes it hard to relax and play in relationships. It also fails to teach him ways of assuring that his emotional needs will be met. The adult child often spends the rest of his life trying to achieve security and power by working harder and harder for less and less return.

We learn at an early age to become excited about "presents." At Christmas and birthdays we combine closeness, food, and material gifts for a child's ultimate experience of feeling loved. The combining of eating and material fix-orientation with family intimacy serves to enhance the meaning of both food and material items.

If families regularly use alcohol in celebrations, children often develop a strong desire to participate in that part of the family fun. If so, they eagerly anticipate reaching the appropriate age. There may be a family tradition of both working hard and drinking hard. The children will learn this in several ways. Perhaps there are specific rituals centered on drinking. Finally, we may have a family tradition of making excuses for past and current family members who are unfortunate enough to suffer from obvious addictions.

## When Daddy's an Addict

Not all are fortunate enough to have their first experiences with fix-oriented behavior be enhancement experiences. Some of us have even more powerful influences than the norm, a family history in which addiction is more than a coping style. It is a way of life. Families in which there are active addictions can greatly magnify each member's reliance on an addictive coping style.

The role models that parents provide for their children are powerful influences. Until about age twelve, each child places faith in his or her parents to set values. While this changes during the teenage years and the peers become more important, parents again assume prominence in early adulthood. When a parent uses regular addictive behavior, the children will see that behavior as one option for the rest of their lives. In learning the addictive coping styles, a child also learns the beliefs which support this coping style. What's worse is the child fails to see more effective ways of believing and of coping with life's problems.

For example, the adult child of chemically dependent parents, in spite of all the negative feelings he has about the parent's addictions, has limited awareness of coping options except to develop addictions of his own. He simply sees no other alternatives. And having poor options is better than no options. This is a painful trap which produces feelings of anger, helplessness, and frustration. The adult child has no awareness of ways to cope with these feelings except through the self-treatment of addiction.

Severe patterns of addiction occur most often in persons from heavily addicted families. These "adult children" begin earlier than normal in the pain-treating process. For them, and others in severe problem families, painful emotions are constant, and seem normal. These persons have great pain at an early age, and begin following the family pattern of self-treating as a primary coping style.

Even in an addictive family, the addictive behavior has its roots in childhood experiences which are very gratifying for the individual. This is one of the reasons an addictive behavior feels so irrationally good to an addict. The addiction serves to remind the addict of an earlier, safer feeling we would all occasionally like to recapture. This is a self-perpetuating trap. We are seeing more and more proof that persons with the highest risk of addiction are those who are born to, and raised by, addictive adults.

**Family Genetics**

One of the most startling findings of research on addictions and families is that genetic factors keep showing up as the most important variables in food, alcohol, sex, and other addictions. In some studies, environmental factors showed no significant influence on whether children born to parents with severe addictions would also develop those same addictions. The newest research shows that children of addicts are also more vulnerable to other addictions. For example, it now appears that sons of alcoholics are excessively vulnerable to cocaine addiction.

In the alcoholism field, we are focusing on informing families of their children's high-risk status for developing alcoholism. We have stated for years that alcoholism is a family disease. When we first began using the family disease concept, many of us only considered the contemporary environments of alcoholic families. Now there is strong evidence that children of alcoholics also have a genetic attribute which makes them likely to develop that disease.

There are parallel developments with obesity, including double-blind studies showing that children of obese parents develop obesity at the same rate whether raised by their natural parents, adoptive obese parents, or adoptive thin parents.

The genetic makeup of a person is the foundation upon which he builds his coping skills and strategies. Favorable attributes such as intelligence, athletic ability, temperament, and physical strength bestow more options than mental retardation, physical handicaps, and other mental and physical dysfunction. We can now add that having a family with a history of certain addictions means one is born with fewer options for enduring addictive coping.

Once we realize that addictive behaviors are never successful paths to meaning, we tend to become less concerned about our addictive potential. However, there needs to be an awareness of the range of options in each of our lives and the effects family addictive patterns have on those options.

## The Outcome

All the above social factors allow addictive coping to flourish. More and more people are pursuing fixes to make themselves happy. Many escape major problems in their lives because their perception does not focus on this fix-orientation. But many who have followed this false path to meaning are having severe problems.

We do not achieve happiness by pursuing fixes. The best we can hope to achieve is temporary need satisfaction. Once the need is met, we go back to having neutral feelings. Happiness is not achieved by catering to short-term emotional demands. Yet, at the heart of both the logical reasoning and the meaning searches in our society is the belief that one can be happy this way. Our official paths to meaning include a series of myths about "the good life." These myths are based on false perceptions and inappropriate fear. This produces self-centeredness and emotional isolation from those we love most.

Since these false beliefs underlie the motivation for most of our achievements, the pursuit of external trappings seems inescapable. Such pursuit anchors the survival beliefs of the society and proceeds rationally from these beliefs. Yet, since the society believes the addictive mythology, such rationality is madness in disguise.

Persons who fully believe in the pursuit of these myths do indeed become "mad," and their lifestyles become "insane." Yet most of us would hardly admit to ourselves that we believe in this mythology. Still, fix-orientation is so ingrained in our society that it is very difficult to gauge the damage it causes. Yet we see it in addicted people.

For most of my clients, the result was unhappiness. They tried harder and harder to be happy using one fix after another. They lived their lives by following the cultural map of reality in the wrong direction. Most instinctively felt confused. They had vague fears and a sense of being lost. Still, they did as they were taught, using external objects to produce internal peace. Since this produces failure, fear increases.

Some of us have very unhappy lives as the result of our beliefs in this fix-oriented mythology. Many people are becoming casualties of these beliefs. Happily, some of them are finding rituals in addiction treatment and twelve-step programs which help them mature beyond the societal mind-set. Even then, the recovering addict may be confused by the contrast between the beliefs which are central to recovery and the beliefs of his friends and leaders. This adds to the relapse rate, and will cease to do so only when we mature as a society.

*For Your Personal Growth*

*Take a note pad and watch television this evening. Make a note of each time you are encouraged to buy something with a fix-oriented sell. Watch the others in the room and notice their reactions to the commercials. Pay close attention to responses to the food and alcohol advertisements. Who gets up to get something to eat and drink and what do they get?*

*Then, watch the characters in the dramas. Notice which ones of them are too dependent in a relationship for their own good. Which ones drink too much? Notice the obvious addictions modeled for you.*

*Now, notice the more subtle clues. Many of the characters can eat and drink at nice restaurants and not gain weight. What about the general attractiveness level of the actors? How much time is spent in bars? How affluent are the characters, and how ruthless are they in maintaining their wealth? How does your life compare to the characters on television? Is it that exciting?*

*Next time you go to the movies or to a play, notice the same things. How is behavior modeled to you? Is there an addict in the plot? Is "unrequited love" the main theme? Just notice, and you will begin to see how the belief that we need a fix is central to the themes of most of our cultural and personal drama.*

*The next time you are out in public, begin to notice the number of cigarette smokers, overweight people, and inebriated people that you see.*

*Sit or lie in a comfortable position. Close your eyes, and breathe slowly and deeply. Let go and relax. Now look back on your life and remember holidays in your childhood. Remember your feelings at major family gatherings. Was food a central part of these times? Was alcohol? Remember your feelings as you anticipated dinner, as you watched the adults around you drink. Remember the feelings as you anticipated opening presents. What did you learn to feel about food, alcohol, things?*

*Now, take a look at your life today. How do you feel about these things now? Do you like the value you place upon food, alcohol, material items? Do the values you hold in these areas make you happy?*

# MAPS, POWERLESSNESS
# AND CONTROL

*None of us really sees reality the way it is.*
*We see reality the way we are.*
- Earnie Larsen

What is an addict trying to achieve? For several years, this question had haunted me. Many believe that each addiction, whether it be to cocaine, sex, or exercise, functions according to universal organizing principles shared with all other addictions. If this is true, does the addictive cycle itself, have a purpose which is similar in every addiction? Do different kinds of addicts, using distinct behaviors, all produce some generic internal result?

It took several years, several clients, and much anxiety to discover that this question was the easiest one all along. The answer was there in the first step of every self-help program, but it had been so obvious that I had overlooked it. The answer lies in the way we perceive reality.

## Do You Know The Way To San Diego?

Many of us approach life with false beliefs about how to live happy, fulfilling lives. We find ourselves going in the wrong direction, yet can't seem to turn around. We just don't know a different way. We are like someone trying to get from my hometown, Indianapolis, to San Diego by driving northeast towards Boston. We often walk around with the worst instructions possible for reaching our desired destinations. These wrong directions are right here in our heads, in the "maps" or "models" of reality we create.

The idea of people making mental maps and acting as if they are reality is very useful in understanding their behavior. Bandler and Grinder have elegantly described how we create our maps and models using images and memories of the input from our senses of sight, hearing, touch, smell, and taste. Since we can only capture how our own unique sensors present reality, no one is able to create absolutely accurate models. Everyone's maps and models are distorted to some degree.

## Our Maps Versus The Territory

Most of us are unaware that our maps of reality, our beliefs about reality, are not reality itself. To quote Bandler and Grinder, "The map is not the territory." Many of life's problems originate in the things we've done and the decisions we've made while confused about this fundamental principle.

According to their research, everyone relies heavily on hearsay evidence, and from observing others, when creating their own personal maps. Each person is dependent upon the accuracy of the ideas of others and upon the certainty of his own observations. Since five people can witness an event and each one describe it differently, this process is highly subjective. Unfortunately, once someone develops a model in his head, he becomes highly rigid about changing it.

There are frequent opportunities to redraw our maps, but for most it is difficult. A reason may be the early origins of fixed beliefs. Some researchers maintain that almost all our views of reality are set, consistently and rigidly, by the age of nine. While there is some truth to this, the human capacity to change can still overcome these original views. Now let's explore how this modeling or map-making process works.

Try to imagine yourself as a conscious computer. You want to understand reality, but the only way to present reality to you, the computer, is through a keyboard using letters, words, and numbers. How would you perceive the sky, or the ocean? What would the symbols tell you about "salty" and "blueness"? How true and complete could these symbolic images be? Symbolic representations through a keyboard would be unable to convey subtle patterns and aesthetic features of the sky and ocean.

Now, assume you have just added a soundless video camera as an input. It's a very good camera, which allows a computer to see much like the human eye sees. You can now "see" the sky and make a model of it. Still limited, you can only see with the camera, and receive input from the keyboard. Would you, the computer, understand the sky in the same manner as a human? No. You would still lack important inputs. We would have to give you the exact equivalent of a human nervous system for you to "understand" reality the way humans do. Even then, you would fail to create a model identical to that of any one person chosen at random. That's because although human beings all have the same, or similar, input equipment, each develops a drastically different model of reality.

We each tend to believe our own parents, friends, preferred government leaders, media, and other credible sources about the nature of reality, even when it contradicts input from our own observational systems. We share our map of reality with a few others, and work to defend this shared map.

Once our maps are stable, we re-fashion the input coming through the senses to keep the maps consistent. The purpose of manipulating and shaping the new input is to allow us to stay sane. When people are forced to change reality maps too rapidly, mental breakdown can occur. Each model or view of reality needs to be rational, yet flexible in order for a person to stay mentally and emotionally stable. When, as in addiction, the manipulation results in excess rigidity and defense of insane coping, it produces insanity in new forms.

**The Natural Lie**

Awarding high priority to keeping our reality models stable creates problems. It causes each person to rank consistency higher in importance than new data. This is true even when new data could promote changes and improvements in the model. Each person resists information which challenges the current model. Even when the basic assumptions of the model are flawed, attempts are made to force "reality" to fit it.

In other words, unlike computers, we each have the ability to lie to ourselves. Each of us uses this ability to maintain the current model of reality. Doing so makes our models of reality, including our coping strategies, resistant or even immune to feedback. Everyone has several ways of doing this.

One way is to delete new information from our memories as soon as, or right after, it is heard. Most have had the experience of telling someone something and having them not hear it, even though the listener was physically close. When trying to maintain a consistent view in the face of data being presented, one will often look confused, get angry, or simply be unable to listen.

Another way input is changed is to simply distort the data as it is received. What one sees, hears, smells, and feels can be misjudged. Words can be changed, voice tones can be varied, expressions misjudged . . . anything to convince the mind it was right all along. If you have ever told someone that you cared, only to have them say something like, "You're only saying that because you want something," in a serious tone, you have seen this distortion in action.

The third way we change data to keep the maps consistent is to generalize, to make the new data or idea too universal to apply to you. This is revealed when you compliment someone and he or she says, "Oh, you say those things to everyone." We see the same phenomenon when someone presents us with a new idea and we conclude that since everyone believes the way we do, this new idea is obviously wrong.

In short, each of us not only makes maps, but we make rigid maps. And we distort new incoming data in such a way as to rank consistency and predictability over accuracy. This provides illusions of security. We then follow those maps throughout life, believing our maps are reality. Unfortunately, the happiness each receives in life is directly proportional to our ability to redraw these maps when needed. Rigid maps create unhappiness.

The rigidity of personal maps was evident in an experience which occurred during my own therapy. I was attending a marathon group therapy for "family" issues. After relating with the other group members for hours, and discussing the effect my father's workaholism had on my childhood, it came time to receive feedback from the group. One of the members started by explaining that it was obvious to her that I had developed the same addictive pattern as my father and needed to learn to let go and enjoy life. This sentiment was immediately echoed by the others, including the therapist.

After some resistance and then deciding that this many people couldn't be wrong, I looked around and said, "Okay, I guess you're right. I'll work on it." My surprise was genuine when the whole group broke into laughter because, even in learning to play, I had automatically said I'd work. Their feedback had been distorted within my model which said I had to work at everything.

## Organic Versus Machinelike Man

The person expressing an addiction is trying to achieve happiness at a physical or bodily level through direct, fix-oriented action. Inherent in addiction is a firmly established belief in control over self, others, and many aspects of the universe.

The addicted person tries to achieve happiness by repeating, in rituals, fix-oriented behaviors. Such behaviors include the ingestion of external objects (drugs, alcohol, and food), actions which directly produce emotional shifts (thrill-seeking and sex), and manipulating other people (especially loved ones). These behaviors have the shared goal of *changing or controlling the addict's internal feeling state* from discomfort to pleasure. He is trying to be happy by coping with, and manipulating, feeling states, rather than by coping with external reality.

Underlying this pattern are several cultural beliefs or myths. The central mythology is one which sees mankind as machinelike. The machine metaphor divides us into two major parts: mind and body. The purpose of the mind is to direct the body. The mind is the operator, and the body is the machine. This dualistic view ignores the spiritual aspects of man. There are many features of this view, but these six are closely tied to addiction:

1. *the belief that I am a mind and a body, as opposed to the belief that I am a central organic being;*
2. *the belief that I can achieve happiness at a bodily, or physical level through my own direct action (in this view, happiness and pleasure are the same, or at least synonymous);*
3. *the belief in self-control, that the mind has the purpose of controlling the body, and that such control is important;*
4. *confusion between happiness and the creation of desired feelings within the body as the result of self-control;*
5. *that this self-control can be effective in changing undesirable feelings and behaviors on a lasting basis;*
6. *that people are in control of each other and we must control others in our lives in order for our needs to be met.*

These beliefs reflect an adolescent phase of development and a fearful state of mind. The behaviors which stem from these beliefs, being self-focused, produce major distortion in the addict's reality. He or she sees the external world only as that world relates to personal emotions. Maintaining this pattern, the addict treats others as pawns to manipulate. Even while manipulating others, emotional control of self remains the purpose.

## The Self As Universe

Much as earth, before the time of Galileo, was viewed as being the center of the universe, with all other planets and suns rotating around it, the addict views himself as the center of the universe with everyone else rotating around him. He acts upon this faulty map of reality, creating pain for self and others. He fails to recognize this self-centeredness. The addict is more likely to define self as sacrificing and magnanimous. His belief is in personal power over the universe and control over everyone, especially himself.

This is the crux of the problem. The self-centeredness of this view is hard to see when you're unaware of it, but easy to see once discovered. In the addict's view, he is the center of everything, and all rotates around him. In truth, he is one minute part of reality, and hardly at its center. Most addicts follow the self-centered model, although they may appear to themselves and others to be loving.

A good example of this is the work-addicted father. He confuses work and love. To him, loving and working are synonymous. Therefore, he defends his work habits on the basis that this is his means of loving. He and other family members often attack those who make emotional demands on him. He wants to work, and this becomes the center of the family's existence. Often, no one in the family can see this addiction as the cause of the emotional impoverishment they suffer. Yet one parent is virtually absent from the loving interaction of the family, producing an emotional imbalance.

## Core Beliefs Of Addiction

All models of reality are systems of belief. Many beliefs come from data outside of personal experience. Many are learned from others. This is usually how our most important or core beliefs are formed. Someone important to us communicates a fear-based belief. Then something happens which appears to validate that belief. Once the validation occurs, we defend the belief. If the core belief is inaccurate, we will believe a lie.

A core belief is just that, a central belief which serves as part of the foundation of our individual philosophies. There is a recent trend in the addictions literature of identifying core beliefs of persons with one specific addiction and developing theories and approaches designed to change them. Let us follow the trend and explore core beliefs which are at the center of all addictive philosophy. Then, I will identify the core beliefs which are at the center of the philosophies of persons in successful recovery. We will then review the outcome of the different beliefs relative to one's competence, internal feeling state, and interaction with others.

## Going The Wrong Way

The addicted person is pursuing a mistaken path in a quest for meaning and happiness. The motivation is positive. The underlying belief system of addiction, however, leads away from intimacy with others and a sense of one's place in the universe, resulting in isolation and feelings of emptiness which I call *The Void*.

The core belief of someone involved in addictive coping of any kind is that meaning and happiness exist at a bodily or physical level, and are achievable as a result of direct action on a person's part. This belief leads him into a self-focused search for happiness and meaning which produces isolation from others and internal fear.

The search seems rational because the addict's behavior is logically consistent with the assumption that the above beliefs about happiness and meaning are true. If they are true, then it makes sense to obtain happiness by drinking, sex and other pleasures. When viewed closely, however, it becomes obvious that the core belief and behavior are irrational because the result is all wrong. By constantly focusing on oneself in a coping strategy, reality itself isn't changed.  The process looks like this:

*False Belief-- >  Self-Absorbed Behavior-- >Isolation-- >Fear*

The fear leads in turn to:

*-- >More Self-Absorbed Behavior-- >More Isolation---- >Fear*


The addict coming into treatment may by surrounded by people, but emotional isolation, internal fear, and behavioral madness are inevitably the outcomes of acting on these false beliefs. The addict acts in a constantly self-focused manner, rather than lovingly, and creates unloving relationships with significant others. Because this is the opposite of the expected outcome, his internal world becomes incoherent. There is no perception that his world makes sense. Active loving is absent in this coping approach.

**Going The Right Way**

Persons recovering from an addiction, especially if participating in a twelve-step program, develop the core belief that happiness and meaning occur at a love or spirituality level, as a side-effect of dedicating oneself to a *power greater than ourselves* and to others in interdependent relationships. Inherent in this belief is both a non-physical concept of meaning and happiness and a need to achieve these outcomes *indirectly*, through connection with the universe.

This belief system leads a person to seek out others, act lovingly toward them, and feel connected with them in interdependent relationships. It also reduces fear and replaces it with feelings of trust and love. The process looks like this:

*New Belief--> Connecting With Others-->Friendships--> Trust*

Trusting in others usually leads to:

*-->More Connectedness-->Spirituality-->Love*

Acting this way produces a sense of coherence, building appropriate relationships with others and a perception of reality which is consistent, predictable, and reliable. In short, a perception of reality develops which *makes sense*.

It is easy to see the direction of the recovery path and contrast it with the addictive one. None of our contemporary paradigms of mental health are consistent with the addictive core beliefs. I am aware of no legitimate approach to mental health that conflicts with the recovery core beliefs model. As you continue to read, it will become easier to see how addictive behavior arises from the addictive core beliefs. It will also become clear that changes in these beliefs are necessary for an addict to achieve the "serenity" referred to in self-help programs.

**"The Void" and "The Nova"**

The core feeling of addiction is fear. The addict presents this feeling in many ways to himself and others and it is easy to misunderstand the motivations involved. There is always, however, a fearful feeling underlying addictive behavior. Giving in to fear does nothing to reduce it. Instead, giving in seems to validate fear.

As a result of this core feeling, the symptom of pain, not its cause, is the constant focus of coping. After addiction develops, it becomes a mechanism for creating much of the addict's pain, which he then treats with more doses of addictive behavior.

In my experience, the addicted person may exhibit pleasure-seeking behavior no matter what his internal feelings are at the time. There are, however, two polar feelings that my clients describe. One is a feeling of great emotional emptiness, which they will agree feels like an emotional black hole they can never fill. I call this feeling *The Void*.

The Void is a feeling state that results from the addict's underdeveloped ability to love, and from his constant catering to his own fears. No one can love him enough to make up for the fear and lack of love he feels. He experiences a state of free-floating fear or anxiety which becomes his constant emotional undercurrent.

There are other authors who have developed similar descriptions of this fear. Viktor Frankl describes the Void as an "existential vacuum."  He refers to a feeling of which his patients complained:

> *...namely the feeling of the total and ultimate meaninglessness of their lives. They lack the awareness of a meaning worth living for. They are haunted by the experience of their inner emptiness, a void within themselves; they are caught in that situation which I have called the "existential vacuum."*

Frankl believes that this vacuum is a widespread phenomenon of the twentieth century. He also states that such a vacuum manifests itself mainly in a state of boredom. He goes on to say:

*Moreover, there are various masks and guises under which the existential vacuum appears. Sometimes the frustrated will to meaning is vicariously compensated for by a will to power, including the most primitive form of the will to power, the will to money. In other cases, the place of frustrated will to meaning is taken by the will to pleasure.*

Frankl and I agree that the person who asks what meaning there is in life *for him* is asking the wrong question. It is up to each of us to create that meaning for ourselves through responsible, loving behavior.

The other feeling my clients describe appears at the other end of the scale. They explain it as a feeling of emotional overflow, usually at times of prosperity in some area. They want to "grab for the gusto" to the best of their ability, and feel this need to explode or completely let go as a part of their celebrating. We jokingly call this the *Impending Nova* or simply *The Nova* in treatment.

The Nova results from the same causes as the Void and is a reinterpretation of free-floating anxiety from the perspective of temporary prosperity. This perspective allows the addict to react to his feelings by trying to get his needs met all at once. It is as if no experience can be enough to fill the Void without adding addictive behavior.

While this feeling seems gratifying, it truly shows he has failed to escape his constant fear even during the prosperous moment. He is sure that the fear is the constant and will return shortly. The addictive behavior is an attempt to put off this inevitability. In both feeling states, the addict's fear results in his interpreting his life as one of never having enough, even when he wins. He has to keep behaving addictively to make up for the constant state of fear.

Part of the fear of addiction has a real basis in the damage addictive behavior creates in the addict's relationships with others. The emptiness of the addictive life provides some basis for feeling isolated. Most of us have some difficulty feeling comfortable during long-term emotional isolation. In a more immediate sense, however, this empty feeling is often illusionary. It is a part of the person's model of reality and is maintained by deletion, distortion, and generalization.

As such, it is totally self-focused and created. It is the result of going inward and creating a negative model filled with negative pictures and words which link with corresponding negative feelings. This is a form of *self-induced trance*. The initial experience with this trance usually occurs within one's original family and continues as a coping option whenever similar fear-provoking experiences are encountered. The fear serves as the signal to emotionally withdraw into this self-induced trance.

Patrick Carnes, in his book on sexual addiction, *Out Of The Shadows*, states that such trances are based on addictive rituals and that all addicts have such rituals. The rituals have the purpose of inducing a trance. Addicts use the rituals of their addictions to withdraw within themselves much like a scared animal will return to its den.

The person who is experiencing fear loses the ability to attend to external reality as the fear feelings intensify. A common reaction to fear is to focus internally on the feeling and to try to analyze and control it, which results in a further intensifying of feeling.

Some people have problems, besides their model of reality, which create trance-like states. For example, those with manic-depressive or other forms of affective illness are often unable to experience comfortable feelings no matter how competent their philosophies. This type of illness is often caused by chemical imbalances in the brain. Many with affective illnesses spend years confused about their illness and use chemicals to treat the uncomfortable feelings the illness causes. When these people begin recovery, they will also need to find other means of improving their emotional states. There are also other forms of mental/emotional illness which produce an inability to control one's emotions. Addiction can evolve from improper treatment of any of these illnesses. Most of us, however, needn't concern ourselves with this complication.

The person who is actively involved in addiction will have both external and internal justification for his fears. The addict in recovery, however, has no current external justification for these feelings, yet will often experience the Void feelings spontaneously, years after giving up coping addictively. This reflects the dominance of his original model of reality. Returning to fear-based consciousness brings back the empty feeling.

The recovering person will then experience a desire to return to addictive behavior to counteract the painful feelings produced by the return to internal focus and the Void feelings. He has, therefore, a need to recognize the illusionary nature of this feeling and to learn to focus on external reality, and to act lovingly upon that reality. He needs to do this as soon as the feeling shift begins in order to decrease the risk of relapse.

Alcoholics Anonymous and other twelve-step programs call this trance state a "dry-drunk" and call the fear-based thought system "stinking thinking." Recently, some writers have described the emotional paralysis of this trance as "frozen feelings."

Each of us does the best we know how to in life. The addict, however, is hampered by his map of reality, by core beliefs and feelings which result in a pattern of coping which is incompetent. For some, biochemical problems keep fearful feelings alive. Fear becomes the central focus of the addict's coping strategy and his coping patterns become utterly circular. The core beliefs and fears will remain during recovery and will re-trigger the addictive behavior unless he recognizes it and evokes other alternatives.

## Powerlessness Over Addictions

The idea of powerlessness is the beginning step in the self-help groups which addicts use to get over addiction. A modified quote of the first steps of those organizations is: "We admitted that we were powerless over our addiction - that our lives had become unmanageable." In the second step of these programs, addicts come to believe a power greater than themselves can restore them to sanity. They are also, in the third step, encouraged to turn the care and direction of their lives over to God as they understand Him.

In summary, the first three steps of AA, Al-Anon, and other self-help groups, advise members that they do not have power over their addictions, and that they need to seek help in learning to live their lives without the illusion of personal power.

This issue of power and control is central to the development of, and recovery from, addiction. As a backdrop, the illusion of power is pervasive in our culture. Alcoholics believe they have power over drinking just as their spouses believe they have power over them. Bosses believe they have power over their employees, and all of us believe we have power over our futures.

In her book *Living In The Light*, Shakti Gawain describes the differences between living in this power-centered manner and living a life in which we turn the care of our lives over to a higher power. Ms. Gawain uses the metaphor of an orchestra. We are all players in this orchestra. We can choose to recognize the appropriate notes and directions from the conductor (our Higher Power), or we can play as if we are the only musician there. If we play along with the orchestra, we help create beautiful music. If we play our own music, without regard for the music of others, we appear to ourselves to be powerful. In actuality, we are merely inconsiderate, and our music produces disharmony.

When we succeed in changing our mood state by addictive behavior, we tell ourselves that we are powerful, that we are the conductor. We are not. We are merely changing notes with no regard for the music of the world. We control nothing; we merely distract ourselves from reality by changing our mood.

When presenting these ideas to others, the audience often asks whether the ability to create our own maps automatically means that we do control our reality. Isn't this ability itself evidence that we have control? The answer is, "No." Our map-making ability gives no more control or power over reality than the ability to map mountains gives us to move them. This process is inherently passive. We have no more control over others than we have over the mountains.

Being convinced that we have power over the universe does not create happiness or serenity. Based on fear, these power beliefs only achieve illusions of consistency and predictability at the expense of accuracy in our models of reality, including that part of the models we consider "ourselves." These power beliefs systematically blind us to the parts of reality we fear and avoid.

They keep us from realizing our own responsibility for the madness the fear causes.

Furthermore, one can either focus on controlling or on loving during any moment in his life. Power-based behavior squeezes out loving behavior in a life as crabgrass squeezes out other grasses in a yard. One can act, in a given moment, either out of love or out of a need to control. No one can do both at once.

### The Myth Of Self-Control

In the area of our self-concept it is difficult to realize that the map is not the territory. Each person perceives himself with even more limited sensory input than he has available about others, yet most feel they know themselves better than others know them. We do know *different* things about ourselves than others do, but we primarily know our maps of reality, with the accuracies and inaccuracies present in those maps. This is not equivalent to *knowing ourselves*.

Much of our energies are expended defending these ideas of ourselves. For example, a person who considers himself a good lover will often defend himself vigorously when told that his partner finds their lovemaking unsatisfying. His self-defense prevents him from learning how to become a better lover. The self-concept is a key part of our model of reality and the one we believe in most strongly. Addicts usually take up even more energy in defending their self-concepts than do others.

In any addictive behavior, one forces a change only in the internal perception of reality. Any change forced on reality comes about because of the imposition of self-centered behavior, your "music" on those around you, and because they react to you in a mutual dance. Recovery is about changing perceptions and learning to play and dance *with* others.

When a recovering addict states that he is powerless over his addictions and life is unmanageable, he is making a statement of fact. After realizing that we are map makers, this position should be easier to understand. The addict is powerless over his addictions precisely because he has imbedded those addictions in his map of himself. Each addict views his addictions as part of himself. This is false. His addictions are merely actions centered in his map of himself. The confusion reflects ignorance about our true natures.

I stated earlier that the addict's behaviors are attempts to control internal mental/emotional states with the goal of maintaining constant pleasurable feelings. The addict believes in and tries to achieve self-control. There are two issues here. One is whether self-control exists. The other is whether it is ever a relevant goal in a coping strategy. Self-control is merely a form of *self-tensing*, and it is useless, even harmful, in a coping strategy. There are several challenging questions about self-control, what it does and how it works:

1. *If one, indeed, has self-control, who does the controlling?*
2. *How is that control achieved?*
3. *Who is controlled?*
4. *How can one be both controller and controllee?*
5. *How can one split oneself in two?*

These are perplexing questions. One organism can't become two organisms by a mere exercise of "will." Try as it may, it cannot change its oneness and it simply can't be both controller and controllee.

Disregarding the above questions for a moment, if one has self-control, where is the location of the power that produces that control? Is it located inside? I have no source of power that I generate myself to produce control. Do you? Is such a source of power located outside, in the world? If it is, then we are stuck using an external something to change our feeling states. Each of us can seem to achieve this for short periods by using "fixes" to change from one feeling state to another, but we are more than feeling states!

You will notice that when you hear the command, "Control Yourself!" you will automatically tense in response to the command. Then, if you wish to act in an appropriate manner, you will have to relax before acting. This is because of confusion inherent in trying to do something that you don't know how to do and that can't even be done. The only logical response the organism can make when told to control itself, is to tense itself. That way, it is doing something while it figures out what it needs to do at the time. It has to slow down in working this way and become less efficient, but it can at least convince itself it is complying with the request.

Once my clients relinquish the belief that they should or are even able to control themselves, the beliefs in their specific addictions become more and more ludicrous. They become free to respond to situations by coping appropriately instead of simply trying to control their emotional state.

As described before, self-control, as used by addicts, focuses on the control of feelings. The feelings are the important things to change because they equate short-term pleasure with true happiness. The feelings are the symptoms which must be self-treated by the addictive behavior. Even when they try to change others in an addictive relationship, they do so in order to change the others into objects which exist to help maintain their own sought-after feeling state.

This feeling state is usually linked to earlier experiences to which they had strong emotional reactions. They are trying, through their addictive behaviors, to go back to an instant in time in which they felt secure, alive, or powerful. They are trying to recapture early drinking experiences, sexual experiences, eating experiences, or other experiences *to feel more intensely*. In this way, they are pursuing a double illusion.

After a few very early successes, addicts rarely achieve the feeling state they desire through their addictive behavior. For example, it has often been years since most of my alcoholic clients have had fun drinking, yet they will continue to tell themselves they will have fun every time they drink. They pursue the illusion that alcohol is still a source of pleasure. They maintain the general illusion that they are in control of their feeling state, and the specific illusion that alcohol still produces pleasure for them. They do not receive pleasure, but constantly delude themselves, so that they believe they do. The ritual of drinking becomes a tool in a more basic lie.

Evidence of this delusion is the belief held by almost every addict that their addictive behavior is a "friend." They make this statement to themselves and, as a result, attach feelings of friendship to a self-destructive behavior. A behavior can't be a friend. Only people, and perhaps animals, can serve in that role. As I ask my bulimic clients, "How can overeating and puking be a friend?" I ask alcoholics how drinking can be a friend. Some of them immediately recognize this obvious glitch in their logic and this helps them change.

Temporarily changing a feeling state does not change the reality it is attached to. Feelings always result from running something through one's map of reality and making a judgement about it. Feelings are created solely as a by-product of one's interpretations of reality. Temporarily changing a feeling state, as one does with addictive behavior, merely supports the belief that the feeling is justified and important. If one uses addictions to control neurotic feeling patterns, he strengthens the position of those feelings in his map of reality. If the feelings weren't important and real, they wouldn't need to be controlled.

Addiction is one tool used in the process of maintaining a flawed map and protecting its consistency and accuracy. Whether the addiction is to alcohol, drugs, sex, work, food, gambling, or of several other ritualized behaviors, the addict is using the objects of addiction to maintain his internal reality and does not understand that this is not a productive behavioral pattern.

We never need to be in control of ourselves. And this is a good thing, since self-control is impossible. We only need to *act appropriately*. The more we pay attention to ourselves, the less attention can be paid to present reality. If a coping style orients toward achieving a certain internal state, it can't focus on getting rid of stressors. One can either do something appropriate, or be preoccupied changing the way one feels. You can't do both in the same instant.

Another example of coping options may clarify this point. A client might have a spouse who is simply moody. The client often reacts by feeling anxious and responsible for the spouse's moods. Addictive, controlling, behavior patterns evolve because the client fashions a coping strategy based on trying to avoid anxious feelings, instead of on addressing the actual problem. There are always healthy options. Here is a diagram of this situation:

| Problem | Symptom | Treatment |
|---------|---------|-----------|
| *moody spouse* | *anxiety* | *talk it out* |
| | | *accept moods* |
| | | *therapy* |
| | | *meditate* |
| | | *divorce* |
| | | *drink* |

Only the last response was potentially addictive.  Yet people often fail to choose any of the options except the last one until I confront them in treatment. In the last option, this person is choosing to control his feeling state in a manner that has no chance of addressing the problem. Such a decision is to control oneself, rather than to cope with reality. When we start paying attention to this pattern, it is amazing how many examples we see and know of people who only consider the addictive option.

There is a general misunderstanding of this area of coping in our society and all of us pursue the illusion of self-control at times. The more central this pattern is to one's behavior and thought patterns, however, the more addictive he is likely to become. The choice seems to be one of focusing on reality and dealing with things on a more or less constant basis, or focusing on feelings, with a resulting diminished ability to deal with external reality. As I tell my clients: *Our feelings are not reality, they are merely our feelings. Deal with reality.*

Feelings are clues to the way each of us maps reality and often show us areas in which consistency and predictability have replaced accuracy in those maps. As such, they are often the best indicators of illusion. The stronger one feels about something, the more likely he is to have distortions in his model about the subject. In paraphrasing Richard Bandler, "Every time we are absolutely sure we are right, there is a ninety-five percent chance that we're wrong." Strong feelings are often reflections of the fear of finding that we're mistaken.

One exception to this rule is the feeling of certainty we have when we decide to give up an addiction. Those who have experienced it know the difference between this feeling and the feeling that we have to be right when defending the same addiction.

Feelings are not reality, but rather they are outcomes of maps of reality, with strong feelings being often indicative of illusion. When we are well-grounded in our maps about any issue, we feel calm and relaxed about an attack on our position, not fearful, angry, and defensive. When our feelings become the direct focus of change, we are not focusing on reality. We are focusing on our model of reality and hallucinating that the model is reality itself. This is the key difference between addictive coping and reality-based coping.

Reality-based coping concentrates on changing, as rapidly as possible, those parts of reality that are stressful. Often this means changing a belief so that we can address external realities more effectively. Addictive coping focuses on changing the feelings, or tension produced by stressors, while ignoring the possibility of changing reality or beliefs.

Feelings do change in predictable ways as the result of changing our responses to reality. For example, when the addict gives up his struggles and begins coping effectively, he begins to experience consistent changes in his feeling states. These feelings are a side-effect of competence, rather than the result of self-control of his emotions. They are a relaxing which results from the cessation of insane coping. The tension of maintaining a constant illusion of control is gone and feelings can flow in response to reality, helping give our experience of that reality positive meaning. We learn to feel love, instead of remaining mired in a fear of losing control. These things are seen as possible when we give up the central illusion that we are in control of reality, instead of recognizing that we are merely a part of it.

*For Your Personal Growth*

*Talk with someone close to you about this chapter. See if the two of you can identify times in which the "Void" feeling is especially prevalent.*

*Review your life goals and activities and see if you are involved with things greater than yourself. List those involvements and review honestly the effort you put into each one.*

*Next time you find yourself depressed, see if the feelings are ones of emptiness. If they are, begin finding ways to love others. Notice the changes in your own feelings as a result.*

*If you experience a feeling which you think is the "Void," try focusing on the image of a television screen with a dark blue screen. Now, flash the words WAKE UP! on the screen in bright white letters while yelling it to yourself in your head. If necessary, go off by yourself and yell the words out loud until the feeling shifts.*

*Sit comfortably and think of an area of your life in which you feel in absolute control. Do you feel safe in this area of your life? Now, begin to evaluate the feeling of control. Are there any outside forces which could, perhaps someday, reduce your control? Perhaps age? Death? Have there been incidents in the past in which you didn't feel this area of your life was secure? Is your feeling of control dependent upon the cooperation of another? Is your control affected by that person's mortality? Can you think of any possible situation in which you would not have control of that area of your life? Are you still convinced your control is absolute?*

*Review your life and ask yourself how you attempt to ensure your happiness. Are you comfortable letting events take their natural course, or do you often feel the need to control them? Do you have one or more habitual behaviors which you use to maintain the feelings you want? Do these behaviors involve others? Is there a pattern of giving, or one of making sure that you always receive?*

*Take time within the next twenty-four hours to ask two or more loved ones what they notice about your attempts to be happy. Do they see you as giving as you see yourself?*

*Finally, ask for feedback about what others see as habitual coping mechanisms in your behavior. This can be the best clue to your areas of addiction.*

# RELATIONSHIPS
# and ADDICTION

*Healthy people have healthy relationships.*
- Earnie Larsen

Howard was another counselor's patient in an alcoholism hospital where I worked. The counselor asked me to get involved in the case because he was having trouble understanding Howard's denial system. After meeting with them, I understood his confusion.

## A Backwards Reality

When we began our session with Howard, he started a tirade about the fact that he didn't want to be there and "why wouldn't people leave him alone and let him drink?" His family had committed him to this treatment after finding him among the street people. He was furious about their "cruelty" in denying him the only thing which gave him pleasure. He had been treated for alcoholism approximately thirty times, and "didn't they know he had nothing else to live for anyway?" He was five-foot-seven and weighed ninety-eight pounds. As he talked about drinking, we could see a look on his face which could only express love. He loved the tool he was using in his slow suicide. When he talked of the people who wanted him to live, his look was hateful.

In Howard's reality, drinking in a way which would kill him was loving behavior. The attempts his family made to intervene in this pattern were cruel and sadistic. Even the staff in the hospital were conspiring to keep him from his only source of meaning. He believed that killing himself was self-loving and other's attempts to love him were cruel. He had almost everything in his model of reality backwards. He died within a year of that treatment.

## The Triple Bind

Robin was a bulimic. She had been a bulimic for ten years before I started working with her in treatment. She was very depressed when she appeared in my office. She was gaining weight in spite of purging by vomiting six times a day and was considering suicide because her life was meaningless. When I asked her what would ensure that her life had meaning she answered, "If I could just be thin, I know I would feel good about myself and develop a loving relationship with a man." This was her only guide on her path to meaning.

Later, I asked her what she did to be loving to herself. Her answer, in a tone of voice which indicated I should already know, was, "Why, I eat!" So she ate to express love to herself, thus interfering with the thinness she contended was the only key to meaning in her life. I asked her if she didn't see a contradiction between eating for self-love and trying to stay thin so she would have a meaningful life with a vital relationship. She said, in an angry tone of voice, "Why in hell do you think I throw up?!"

Robin had only one way of nurturing herself in her model of reality. And she had only one strategy for achieving love. Those two ways of operating were in competition with each other, and she balanced them by vomiting up the food she used to love herself, so that someone else would love her. She had no relationship skills, however. Her strategies didn't work and she was killing herself.

Robin has since stopped overeating and has learned the skills she needs to nurture herself properly and to maintain relationships with others. We are still working together, and will laugh at the bind she had herself in. She still has trouble believing her model of reality was so ineffectual.

Both Howard and Robin had extremely distorted beliefs about relationships. They were incompetent in their relationships with themselves and others and were controlled by beliefs which made no sense at all. In some areas, their beliefs were the direct opposite of the truth. This describes, to some degree, the models of reality of every addict I have ever known. Beliefs about relationships are key elements in their distorted models of reality.

**Me, You, and God**

There are three types of relationships: relationships with ourselves, relationships with other beings, and relationships with a Higher Power or God. The addicted person is confused and incompetent in all three of these areas. All addiction is both the cause and reflection of these poor relationship skills. The addicted person doesn't understand what it means to love self, others, and God. He has a poor relationship with himself and his relationships with others will reflect the projection of this problematic relationship outward. His relationship with God will either be non-existent, or he will use God as the scapegoat for all the problems which result from his own incompetence in life.

In another sense, however, all addictions stem from an addictive relationship we have exclusively with ourselves. In an internal addictive relationship, we treat ourselves with no more love than we treat others. We view ourselves as things to be controlled. We manipulate ourselves in hopes of maintaining the experience whose absence we fear. Our external addictive relationships are simply the inevitable result of projecting our internal confusion outward onto the others in our lives. In this manner, all addiction is a reflection of problems in the broad realm of relationships.

Every addiction first reflects a problem within the most important relationship each of us has, our relationship with ourself. Addiction reflects confusion in our definition of ourself and in our definition of love. The addicted person believes that acting in a fix-oriented manner, while problems worsen, is self-loving. Such behavior is sadomasochistic, with the addict playing both the sadist and masochist roles at different times.

In almost every case, when I ask a person with a severe addictive problem if he loves himself, I see a look of confusion. Being a recipient of self-love is usually not in an addict's model of reality. Addicts hear others talk of self-love, but have no idea what it means. The addict's whole quest is to find love or a love substitute in external reality. Loving oneself doesn't fit in that reality.

When projecting this confusion outward into relationships with others, the addict uses others to provide feelings of security, sensation, and power. The addict believes this is loving. He doesn't know the difference between loving and controlling. These relationships also become sadomasochistic, as they reflect the inner confusion of both persons. All addiction arises from this confusion. This confusion must be resolved before addictive patterns can be changed.

The essence of the relationship problem is bewilderment about which behaviors are loving and which are unloving. The alcoholic will see the systematic suicide of drinking as self-loving behavior. When others in his life confront this illusion, he perceives them as cruel and unloving. The compulsive overeater believes that eating is self-loving, at least at the time of the decision to eat. The sex addict believes that sex, whether occurring in a loving relationship or not, is the most important evidence of giving and receiving love. This will often occur even when he is molesting a child. The pedophile will often see this, one of the cruelest behaviors imaginable, as the most loving act possible towards the child.

In short, the love dimension of the addict's reality models are the direct opposite of the truth. While harboring these backward beliefs, in every case they see systematic emotional and physical suicide as loving behavior and see loving attempts to bring them back to reality as cruel and insensitive.

Addictive behavior itself is never loving, regardless of its form. It is never loving for an alcoholic to cope by drinking. It is never loving for a sex addict to share in cold, unloving sexuality; neither is it loving for a food addict to indulge in rich desserts. In none of these instances is the addictive behavior nurturing the person's real needs or increasing his competence.

Projected outward toward others, confusion and incompetence often produce a *relationship addiction*. In a relationship addiction, each person confuses which behaviors are loving and which ones are cruel, and each uses the other as "objects" to medicate the anxieties which result from having a distorted internal belief system about love.

## A Modern Tragedy

A friend of mine recently killed himself. His death struck deeply at many of us in the community, even those who didn't know him well. We wanted to know what happened. We needed to know what happened.

My friend had always had a tendency to drink too much. In recent years, he had drunk on a regular basis, but hadn't, to my knowledge, shown very bizarre behaviors. He and I shared problems of work and food. We would meet for lunch on a regular basis and share our progress or lack of progress on these issues. At the time of his death, it had been several months since we had met for lunch. I wasn't concerned then, however, as he had recently married and he and his wife worked in the same building.

As his friends tried to solve the puzzle of his suicide, it became obvious what had occurred. His co-workers found notes in his desk dating back five years or so. In all the notes, the theme was the same. He had thought of killing himself because of his failure in relationships. One of our mutual friends had talked to him just before his death about problems he was having in his marriage. She said he and his wife were fighting often about her need to control his time. Also, they had gone on a spending spree during the first nine months of their marriage and were deeply in debt. The friend was concerned, primarily because of the debt issue. This was always a sore spot. She had no idea of the depth of his insecurities about relationships.

When we pieced together the puzzle, we found that he had been depressed over the relationship, drinking more, and taking diet pills to deal with his weight. At his funeral, another friend stated it was the chemicals which led him to the act, but I disagreed, saying it was his long-term difficulty with relationships which had been the core problem.

My friend and his new wife were both relationship addicts. They were using each other in their marriage as sources of security, sensation, and power. They each had other addictions, too. His were food, alcohol, and work. Hers were spending and religion. The intensification of the relationship addiction also resulted in binges in their other addictions.

As in most relationships of this type, my friend saw his wife as a source of nurturing, especially sexual, while she saw him as a source of status and security. The suicide was precipitated when he began to see the sickness in the relationship and thought about ending it. She countered by going off birth control, lying to him about still being on it, and getting pregnant. Her last power move was to try to assure that he would remain a status object by trying to bind him with a child. His last power move was to take himself out of the game, permanently.

## Relationship Addiction and "Co-Dependence"

One of the major developments in the past fifteen years in the addictions field is the increasing knowledge about these relationship addictions. There are two major approaches to addiction. One approach is to describe certain close, romantic relationships as addictions and detail how this works. The other approach is to define all addictive relationship patterns as "co-dependence" and present a broader model of how we learn to use our relationships with other people to "medicate" our feelings.

As I have worked with this issue, it has become apparent to me that relationship addictions serve as the glue which holds together all the other addictive patterns. No matter what other addictions a person has or has had, every addicted person has, as a central life pattern, controlling, fix-oriented relationships with other human beings. These relationships serve to give *pseudo-meaning* to an otherwise meaningless existence, and to provide at least a tenuous tie to external realities.

The only exception to this rule is when another addiction, like alcohol, demands too much time and energy for the addict to maintain these relationships. The first thing that an addict in recovery from such an addiction will try to do so is establish an addictive relationship!

We all have seen relationship problems lead someone to behave in bizarre ways. Relationships are the cause of our greatest happiness and our greatest pain. Pain usually arises when we are approaching relationships addictively. Relationship addiction kills just as effectively as other addictions, and is part of every person's life who is addicted in other ways. Relationship addiction is the most dominant and enduring feature of the lives of most addicts.

My approach is to consider the ideas of relationship addiction and co-dependence in combination. Both these ideas pertain to our addictive romantic relationships, and to all other relationships which provide feelings of security, sensation, and power. It is important to recognize, however, that each external addictive relationship is a "co-dependent" relationship in that it "takes two to tango." I frequently see large groups functioning on a foundation of interlocking addictive relationships. We simply can't have an addictive relationship with another without that person's cooperation. The term *co-dependence* is also appropriate for such relationships.

In external addictive relationships, we are always trying to exploit the behavior, feelings, and thoughts of others in a self-centered manner so that we can use our interaction to "medicate" our own uncomfortable feelings. Others are objects to be used, instead of persons to be loved. From our childhood relationships with our parents to the conglomeration of relationships we have in our adult lives, we are often in this dance of addiction.

We rehearse addictive relationship patterns in our families of origin and perform them in our romantic, parenting, friendship, work, and other relationships. Robert Subby, who uses the "co-dependence" term to describe this addiction states that co-dependence is:

*The denial or repression of the real self based on an erroneous assumption that love, acceptance, security, success, closeness, and salvation are all dependent on one's ability to do "the right thing."*

I would add that "the right thing" is the behavior which the co-dependent believes will ensure either security, sensation, or power. Subby's definition makes it clear that co-dependence stems from and produces confusion about the real self and about real needs. As every addict has addictive relationships as one of the addictions in his life, every addict suffers from this co-dependent denial of the real self.

Relationship addiction creates problems which we often treat with other addictive behaviors. We also use our relationship addictions to justify other destructive addictions, saying "we deserve" to drink, drug, or have sex excessively because our parents, wives, children, or employers are so unreasonable.

Both men and women practice addictive relationships. Historically, women have learned models of establishing relationships in which they act dependent, but control from moral postures. Men have learned to complement this role by attempting to control from positions of power. These traditional definitions are breaking down, but the contest continues, only with less restrictive choreography. There is a constant power struggle, with each sex using different forms of power for which the other sex has few effective forms of defense. Such interaction drives a wedge between the combatants.

Almost all domestic homicides arise out of addictive relationships. Child abuse is an expression of a set of addictive family relationships, as are spouse abuse and sexual victimization. On the milder side, the person who becomes very depressed after the break-up of a romantic relationship and feels as if his world is meaningless is going through withdrawals from this addiction. This is obviously our most frequent addiction.

Relationship addictions are exciting at first, but create immense pain later. One of the purposes of addictive relationships is to provide support for the other addictive coping options practiced by both parties in the relationship. In its most severe forms, relationship addiction is injurious to all involved. These severe addictions are prevalent and virtually create a need for much of the mental health field. People often murder the spirits and bodies of those they profess to love the most.

## "True Love"

Addictive relationships are often considered the normal romantic relationship. Even our institutions of marriage teach us that two halves become whole. I am particularly fond of Anne Wilson-Schaef's definition of this type of addictive relationship. She states:

> *An addictive relationship is the basic relationship within our culture. It is a "cling-clung" relationship. Both persons involved are convinced that they cannot exist without it. They see themselves as two half-persons who must stick together to make a whole. They arrive at decisions in tandem. They practically synchronize their breathing. We are taught from an early age to call the addictive relationship by another name: true love.*

So the relationship-addicted person sees himself or herself as half of a whole who needs another person to be complete. This way of approaching relationships doesn't work well and fosters much pain. The truth, as Robert Subby has said, is that *when you multiply one-half times one-half you end up with one-quarter.* We may not enter our romantic and parental relationships feeling like a whole person, but we have the responsibility to ourselves and our loved ones to become one.

The mechanical equal of a person who is addictive in relationships is a vacuum cleaner. These go around trying to be loved instead of loving, thinking they are loving when they are acting as emotional sponges. They are confused about love, and think they are loving when they are really involved in addictions. They mistake the intense feelings produced by this addiction for love.

Drs. Cowan and Kinder point out, in *Smart Women/Foolish Choices*, that the relationship addict confuses longing with love. I believe this longing is a fear-based hunger for security, sensations, and power. The feeling the relationship addict often identifies as love is, instead, fear.

Addictive relationships are long-term prostitution contracts, which state, "I'll meet your wants, if you'll meet mine," with each person trying to be sure that his wants get met the best. In spite of this selfishness, relationship addicts are masters at depicting themselves to self and others as victims whenever their wants aren't fulfilled.

If you are an adult living with another adult who is clearly an addict, assume, until proven otherwise, that you are just as much an addict as your addictive complement. In almost every case, you will be correct in this assumption. Should you view yourself as a victim in the relationship, you can be absolutely sure that you are an equal in the process. You can also believe that your relationship with that person is one of your addictions. This is usually a good place to start recovery.

This is especially true of the relationship addict involved with someone who has a debilitating substance or behavioral addiction. This "co-dependent" person is often furious at the other person, blaming him or her for any unhappiness in the relationship and family. The anger of the co-dependent toward the other addict is part of a relationship addiction, and is based on the co-dependent's desire to be the center of the other addict's universe, and the resentment felt when it doesn't happen.

This resentment is usually expressed by the statement that the co-dependent loves the other addict more than the other addict loves him. This feeling that the co-dependent calls love isn't love. It is the fear-based desperation of someone whose relationship addictions aren't working, and who is looking for someone else to blame for failing to develop a sane coping model.

If you see your primary relationship as the center of your search for meaning in your life, you are probably addictive with that relationship. Loss of awareness of the separation between your feelings and those of the other person is another symptom. The relationship and the rest of your life will be more meaningful if you learn to put the relationship in perspective.

Should you find yourself feeling insecure and fearful about your love relationship, with no real reason for those feelings, then the relationship is showing signs of addiction. If the relationship primarily produces feelings of tension, then positive action should be taken.

## "But I Need A Child!"

Persons in addictive marriages with others who have severe addictions to alcohol, sex, or work often develop addictive relationships with their children as a way of protecting the relationship with the spouse. Members of other types of emotionally constricted families develop these relationships because of their inadequacies in other areas. They misplace dependency needs to their children, and those children can't depend on either parent for consistent emotional support until one or both parents learn to love them appropriately.

Audrey is the adult child of an alcoholic. When she began working with me, it was at the suggestion of her father, who had been in recovery for over two years and was seeing some of his self-focused behavior emerging in his daughter. He knew enough about addictions at this stage to accurately identify some of her problems.

Audrey came in to address her problems in relationships, specifically her marriage. Her husband was also an adult child, and she was sure he was at least as sick as she was. When asked how she felt about her parenting, she assured me that she wasn't "making the mistakes her parents made." As we explored her marital history, however, a different picture emerged. Audrey had addictive relationships with her husband and her children.

During their childbearing years, Audrey and her husband were having their first problems with his family. She felt she couldn't compete with his mother and alcoholic brother. She decided that if she had a baby, she could tilt the scales in her favor. No thought was given to whether it was loving to bring a child into such a marriage. The child was merely a pawn in her addictive marriage.

After the child was born, she threw herself into the role of mother and used the power inherent in that position to get her way by dominating her husband in several types of situations. She stopped having sex and further alienated her husband. Her children were the center of her empty life, and she overprotected them. They were developing neuroses of their own, too.

Audrey and her husband have salvaged their marriage and are doing a decent job of parenting now. There are, however, many people today who are having children when they are not ready because they need an extra pawn to use in the chess game of addictive relationships.

Addiction is contagious. It is transmitted genetically and through learned behavior patterns within families. In families with addictive parents, the parents have a union which is based primarily on fear and the quest for security. At progressed levels of addiction, the fear leads to a hunger for sex and power over one's partner. If either parent has an addiction besides this one, then the relationship will also be addictive. This will affect the children.

The children of relationship addicts grow up in a home in which the parents are unable to love each other consistently. The parents think they love each other very much because they confuse intensity of feeling with loving feelings, but the intensity reflects fear, not love. These children often have various behavioral problems which reflect attempts to cope with this fear. In addition, the relationship addiction drains off the energy the parents need to consistently love their children.

If you are overly involved with children, and have problems disciplining them because you fear they will learn to dislike you, then the parent-child relationship is addictive and unhealthy. Another prime symptom is spending a good deal of time imagining negative things happening to them, creating fear and worry. If you had children because you needed them, or feel that your mental health depends on your children, the addiction is potentially destructive.

Other people, especially children, are not meant to be objects to provide our security, sensation, and power fixes. When we marry, have children, raise children, or interact in any dishonest way with others with the purpose of stemming feelings of fear and insecurity, we are being cruel to ourselves and others. We need to identify the positive, loving potential within ourselves and develop relationships which are expressions of that potential.

**Learning Our Addictions**

When children are raised in addictive homes, they learn to be addictive themselves. Most persons with severe addictions come from homes in which there were severe addictions. Depending on the addictive pattern, several bizarre patterns can evolve which form the foundation for problems later. Earnie Larsen states that *what we live with, we learn; what we learn, we practice; and what we practice, we become.* This is a very elegant way of describing how we learn coping methods. We become much like our parents in a coping sense because we are exposed to them on such an intense basis as children.

More important, however, is the antithesis of Larsen's statement: *what we don't live with, we don't learn, practice, or become.* Children of addictive parents fail to learn positive self-esteem and loving behaviors because the parents themselves lack these qualities. When children are in addictive relationships with their parents, they are victimized in two ways. First, they develop histories which teach them fearful ways of thinking, acting, and feeling. Second, they fail to see successful coping mechanisms. The greatest area of failure is usually in the area of understanding and being able to practice truly loving behaviors.

Children of addicts learn to look for behaviors which are "right" behaviors within the context of an addictive environment. When they use these behaviors to cope with the world of other adults, the consequences are terrible. The only thing a life in an addictive household prepares us to do as adults is to find others who were also from addictive households with whom we can recreate our addictive families.

The core of recovery from addictions is to develop the ability to love ourselves and others consistently. The twelve steps practiced in self-help groups teach us to do that. Good therapists help us do that. Once we learn this, it becomes obvious that practicing an addiction is never a loving thing. Throughout our recovery, we come back to relationships. We have to heal this area in order for other areas to prosper.

## The "Higher Power" Relationship

The most difficult relationship for those who cope addictively is the one which reflects the broad category of spirituality. Whether we use the western ideas of God, or any of several other concepts, the addicted person feels isolated from any loving force of the universe. He is spiritually bankrupt because the addictive lifestyle is inherently non-spiritual. Conversely, recovery from addiction is inherently spiritual.

M. Scott Peck makes the point in his book *The Road Less Traveled* that we develop our images of God largely through interaction with our parents. If we have parents who are loving, we picture a loving God. If we have parents who are cruel, judgmental, and selfish, we tend to picture God the same way. Given the number of addicts who were themselves parented in an addictive manner, it is not difficult to understand how they have a difficult time relating to their original image of a higher being.

Yet, spirituality is a much broader area of our lives than our feelings towards a higher being. It also includes and usually operates around our feelings towards each other. It is in this area that addicts usually work toward learning to feel included in the universe again. They see others who have achieved serenity in their lives which they admire. This leads them to learn from the others who have already worked through this issue.

Most members of self-help groups feel that this is the most important element in recovery. I agree. Relationship addiction leads us to feel more and more isolated from others and from whatever loving forces exist. Recovery is incomplete until we feel a part of humanity and the universe in a positive, forceful way.

## Capable, But Not Lovable

When Bill came to see me, it was because of "stress." He was always tired, and realized that he worked too much. As he and I talked, it was obvious that Bill had spent his whole life trying to compensate for feelings of being unlovable, which he developed in his alcoholic family, by being super-capable. He was wealthy, and had four children, two of whom were in college. His wife was physically beautiful, and he couldn't understand why he no longer desired her sexually. He worked sixty hours per week, volunteered in several organizations, and coached his youngest son's soccer team. He was admired for his capabilities.

One of the first things that I pointed out to him was that he was incompetent in over fifty percent of the skills he needed to have a happy life. And he had been making himself more incompetent in those areas for years. When I explained that I knew that he felt he was a phony, and had felt this way for years, he decided to stay in my office and listen to the rest of my explanation.

Bill had never learned how to love. Feeling totally unlovable himself, he avoided this area of his development and attempted with his many other skills to manipulate others to provide him with security, sensations, and power. He knew he was tired, but he didn't know he was a work and relationships addict. Recently, he had traded a food addiction for an exercise addiction. This had added to his fatigue.

Bill threw himself into the effort to become lovable with the same determination he had always used to solve other problems in his life. Imagine his dismay when he realized that he was so handicapped in this area that it would take him five years just to achieve his first level of goals. He faltered, then started one of the most dramatic healing processes I have ever seen.

His wife, Pat, had always loved him. She had grown up in a healthy environment, and had been instrumental in helping the children understand and accept their father. Bill had several people who genuinely cared for him, but because he didn't know he was lovable, he couldn't feel it.

He and Pat started with their relationship. She was delighted when he finally started talking about his lagging sex drive. She had begun to question her own attractiveness. It turned out that he had been trying to go directly from his harried mind-set into lovemaking without any time to reconnect on an emotional basis. His recent exercise schedule had also increased his fatigue. I prescribed that he stop running and start walking, with his wife. They used the walking time to talk about their relationship, and were able to let things flow from there.

Over the next two years we included his children, his parents, and her parents in the recovery process, and the warmth in this family was remarkable. His oldest son dropped out of college and became a carpenter after Bill realized how he had pressured him to go to college, denying his son's desires to work with his hands. His youngest son gave up soccer after he confessed he had only been doing it as a way of getting some of his father's time. They took up fishing. Many other healthy changes occurred.

Finally, Bill addressed his long-term fear of religion. The nuns in a Catholic grade school had abused him and he became phobic about religion and spirituality. While he never joined a church, Bill became one of the most loving, spiritual men I have ever known. He grew to appreciate the intimacy in his life more than most of us because he had been starved for it most of his life. He is now fifty, retired, and living out west in the mountains.

Bill's recovery is unique, but not that unique. Those of us who have lived for years in the emptiness of addictive relationships have an untapped hunger for health which prompts us to value healthy relationships, once we develop them, as the most important things in our lives. We work at intimacy, and the dividends can be tremendous.

In the next chapters, we will explore the other addictions and how the addictive process works. Remember that where you find the other addictions you will find relationships which are addictive and unhealthy. Furthermore, recovery from other addictions will not produce serenity until the relationships heal. Alone, we cannot get well in the lovability areas of our lives.

*For Your Personal Growth*

*Relax for a moment and picture your father expressing emotions. What emotions did he show throughout the time you were growing up? Now, repeat this process, picturing your mother expressing emotions. Once you have a clear memory of your mother's expression, combine the two sets of memories, your mother's and father's expressions of emotions.*

*Now ask yourself what emotions you express. How much broader is your range of emotional expression than the combined expressions demonstrated by your parents?*

*If you are married or in another steady relationship, does your partner remind you of either of your parents? Perhaps a little of both? Do you act similarly to either of your parents in this relationship? Are you happy with the current patterns?*

*If you have children, review the ways in which you parent as your parents did. Were there any parenting behaviors which you hated in your parents which you now find yourself doing?*

*Finally, brainstorm alternatives to any uncomfortable patterns you see in yourself. If you can't think of alternatives, talk to others whose expressions of emotions, relationship patterns, and parenting skills you admire. Let them explain their ways of viewing reality and behavior so you can learn.*

# THE ADDICTIONS

*Addictions are not evil or bad-they just cost you too much in lost perceptiveness, wisdom, effectiveness, and happiness.*
                                                                    - Kenneth Keyes

Even though this book focuses on the central, unifying aspects of the process of addictive coping instead of on distinct addictions, this chapter does highlight specific addictions so that you can recognize patterns in your own life and see how addiction works. In the last chapter, I explored relationship dependence and will exclude it from discussion here, except in instances where it is relevant to the addiction being discussed.

This chapter begins with those addictions that are societally sanctioned, or approved, and proceeds to those which are not well understood or accepted. I hope this approach will help you expand the way you think about addictive behavior. Other authors such as Earnie Larsen, Lawrence Hatterer, Kenneth Keyes, Anne Wilson-Schaef, Patrick Carnes, and Shakti Gawain are using similar sketches of the addictions described here. We all recognize the same behaviors and agree, for the most part, about the ingredients of a central addictive process.

All societies distinguish between acceptable or "good" addictions and unacceptable or "bad" ones. In our society, there are some clear distinctions. We are inspired to acquire and maintain certain addictive patterns so that we are more useful, in a machinelike sense, to society. The society prizes these addictions because they spring from some of the noblest of human ventures, and disturb one's life only when practiced excessively.

In her writings, Anne Wilson-Schaef also contrasts substance or ingestive addictions, which are dependence on something which can be ingested, and process addictions, which are addictions to a specific series of actions or interactions. This is a useful distinction. You will see both good versus bad and ingestive versus process distinctions here.

## "Good" Process Addictions

The process addictions normally thought to have positive value in our society are relationship, work, religion, materialism, exercise, and worry. All these have a positive value in moderation, but can cause problems when used as a primary coping response. Relationships were covered in the previous chapter. This chapter describes the others.

*Work Addiction*. One of the most common addictions, and the one least recognized as a problem, is work addiction. The feelings of a client's mother when she heard from my client that some of the family's problems were related to father's work obsession and responded, "Well, at least that's a good addiction," are common. Actually, work addiction is potentially fatal and we need to recognize it as such.

The need to work, to contribute to the common good and to our own survival is one of the noblest human needs. We classify people as saints because of their work for mankind. Where would civilization be without those who have added to it by their work? Likewise, where would each of us be if someone hadn't put forth the effort to assure our survival in our early years by working. Work is also, however, a means by which we practice unloving needs for security, sensation, and, especially, power. It is work in that context which can be addictive and destructive.

The following story from *Work and Love: The Crucial Balance*, by Dr. Jay B. Rohrlich illustrates this point.

The story of a friend of mine is a painful illustration of the importance of knowing what the role of work in our lives is all about. He died of a sudden heart attack while on vacation with his wife in the Caribbean. He was a man of apparently robust health and limitless energy until that day when he lay on the warm beach looking into a cloudless sky. Chief of surgery at a major metropolitan hospital, he maintained a large private practice, commuted from a house in the suburbs, wrote and published extensively, and attended frequent professional meetings locally and throughout the country. He was rarely home before nine in the evening and began work at seven each morning, which necessitated his leaving his house by five-forty-five.

He enjoyed the two-and-a-half-hour daily commute because it enabled him to read and write on the train. He resented sleep as unproductive. His weekends were packed with home-based projects when he wasn't attending conferences or writing. He once told me that as Fridays approached each week, he would inevitably experience mounting tension if he had to anticipate forty-eight hours of unstructured time. This would be diminished if he had several projects to look forward to, such as building a tree house with the kids, rotating the tires on his two cars, or mowing his forty thousand square feet of Kentucky bluegrass lawn.

As Sunday evening came, the heavy burden of weekend leisure began to lift, and by Monday morning, he admitted that he virtually sailed into his office or the operating room with a sense of thrill and challenge. He admitted that he made halfhearted complaints about how hard he worked, how badly he wanted to spend more free time with the family, and how he longed to travel with them, but he knew that he really could not.

In fact, he always had reasons for being unable to take more than a few days vacation each year with the family. His wife became accustomed to spending most vacations waiting for her husband to extricate himself from some urgent problem which inevitably arose to destroy their plans.

*Or he would seem to "get sick" before or during the vacation. When he did get away, much of his time was spent on the telephone, or writing or reading important professional material.*

*The year he died was going to be different. He promised his wife, who was becoming quite depressed herself, and had given him a gentle ultimatum, that he was going to take a three-week vacation in the true sense of the word. After his death, many of his friends and family members agreed that his heart simply could not sustain such a driving, punishing work pattern.*

*The question, however is: What really killed him? Was it the work, or was it the vacation? He was literally phobic about time he spent that had no fixed purpose, no defined end point or "product", and time that had no organization involving a regular sequence of skillful activities. Evenings at home, weekends, vacations, and thoughts of retirement were anguishing, disorienting experiences for him unless he was "meaningfully" occupied. Is it not possible that for him the enforced "relaxation" of the vacation proved to be lethal?*

Dr. Rohrlich goes on to describe the deeper dynamics of work, leisure, and the competition in one's life between time spent working and time spent in loving interaction with others. I recommend his book highly.

In the pattern of work addiction, as that in the example, a person learns early in life that he is important as the result of working hard. Later in life, some use work as a strategy to cope with problems. Take the following example:

| Problem | Symptom | Treatment |
|---|---|---|
| *Intimacy Problems* | *Anxiety* | *Work* |
| *Boring Marriage* | *Depression* | *Work* |
| *Discomfort as Parent* | *Anxiety* | *Work* |
| *Failure in Business* | *Depression* | *Work* |

This person responds to all tensions by going back to work. Everyone may admire him except those close to him who feel neglected.

The work addict usually develops more than one addiction through a progressive process. An addiction to work creates great fatigue and requires offsetting addictive strategies to treat this "hangover" feeling. A common pattern is to develop a gambling or sex problem, or both. For example, there is the male work addict who experiences exhaustion and decides to go to Vegas with some of his associates for a "break." He loses too much money, uses the hookers, and has to work extra hours to "make it up to his family." In essence, he "progresses" in his addiction:

| Problem | Symptom | Treatment |
|---|---|---|
| *Intimacy Problems* | *Anxiety* | *Work* |
| *Boring Marriage* | *Depression* | *Work* |
| *Discomfort as Parent* | *Anxiety* | *Work* |
| *Failure in Business* | *Depression* | *Work* |
| *Work Addiction* | *Fatigue* | *Gambling* |
| | | *Sex* |
| *Money Loss* | *Guilt* | *Work* |

Here we see how a single addictive behavior leads to movement, a progression through the addictive process. Addicts have an uncanny ability to come back to coping choices which continue their addictions. They even make mistakes which only their addictive behavior seems to fix.

Work addiction is the most socially instilled addiction, especially for males. It also has a tendency to remain in a person's coping arsenal after he has dropped most other addictions, even though it creates almost no pleasure for most people. Having a work addiction is almost a badge of honor which seems, to the addict, to make it acceptable for him to have those other "nasty" habits.

*Religion Addiction.* Another "good" addiction is religion. Earnie Larsen, in his book *Stage II Recovery*, states:

> *When you make a god of religion, you abuse the very nature of religion. When, in the name of religion, you give up your responsibilities to think, decide, and act, you are not being "religious." Passivity isn't a sign of spirituality.*

Anne Wilson-Schaef, again, has an excellent description of the religion addict:

> *Religion can also be a process addiction. I am not talking here about being religious or being spiritual. Rather, my concern is with "quick-fix" religions, those that avoid thoughtful prayer, meditation, and dialogue and claim to have all the answers.*
>
> *The religion addict is someone very different, inside and out, from the person involved in spiritual growth. The religion addict loses touch with personal values and develops behaviors that are the same as those of the alcoholic or drug addict: judgmentalism, dishonesty, and control. Use moves into abuse.*

Our need to feel connected with something greater than ourselves underlies all our religious traditions, is noble, and can result in things quite wonderful. From Christ's healing the sick to Mother Theresa's work with the poor of the world, our highest acts of love spring from the center of our spiritual beings. It is possible, however, to use the dogmatic aspects of religion as a means of obtaining security and illusionary higher status than others with different beliefs, or even than others with the same beliefs whom we judge to follow those beliefs imperfectly. It is primarily this power-centered use of religious belief which is addictive.

Much pain can be created in a family when one or more parents attempt to be loving parents by practicing addiction to religion. In families in which a person copes solely by religious means, the exact same patterns exist that exist in the work addictive and the alcoholic families.

We can take the example from the work addict, change the treatment, and see similarities.

| Problem | Symptom | Treatment |
|---|---|---|
| *Intimacy Problems* | *Anxiety* | *Pray, preach Bible* |
| *Boring Marriage* | *Depression* | *Pray, preach Bible* |
| *Discomfort as Parent* | *Anxiety* | *Pray, preach to kids* |
| *Business Failure* | *Depression* | *Pray, read Bible* |

This is a mild example. I have one case of a married couple, one of whom is alcoholic, the other addicted to her "Christianity." The husband is dealing with his addiction well, but his efforts to rebuild his marriage are blocked by his wife's addiction to her religion and their relationship addiction. She is, and always has been, emotionally distant. Whenever someone asks about her feelings about something, she answers that her religion states that she is to feel a certain way, and that is how she feels. Her facial expression and the rest of her body language state that she is in pain, but she uses her religion as a barrier against both love and hate because of her fear of being imperfect.

In recent years, there has been publicity about religious"cults" which have overpowering psychological influences on their members. Therapists have developed a treatment called "reprogramming" to help the family of a cult member get the member to re-enter the family and society. This type of experience is another example of addiction to a religious system. The security, sensation, and power/powerlessness dimensions mentioned earlier permeate these cult environments.

One of the recent self-help groups for troubled members of "fundamentalist" churches, called Fundamentalists Anonymous, is receiving much attention. The need for options for persons with religious addictions is great, but it is crucial not to demean anyone's religious convictions.

In approaching religious addiction, the important question is whether the religious person is motivated by love of God and others, or whether the religion is simply an instrument of a fear-based search for security, sensation, and power to bully others. The difference between these motivations is usually clear when you study a case carefully. In my experience, highly loving, religious people engender love and hope in others. Religion addicts breed guilt and fear. It is usually simple to tell the difference between these two types of persons by our internal feeling responses to them.

Sometimes, however, it is difficult to tell if a charismatic religious leader is truly spiritual or someone practicing an addictive lifestyle and using religion to gain power. The incidents of Jonestown and the television evangelist scandals of 1988 illustrate the negative power of this addiction.

*Materialism Addiction.* The desire for objects, while not one of our noblest reactions, can be seen nearly everywhere in our society. We can buy food, clothing, shelter, and less-needed items as means of showing our love for others in our lives. We can also give of such items to those in need, whom we do not know personally. The gift of something to make life more enjoyable is fine, but the belief that material items are the major path to happiness and meaning is damaging. Writers throughout the ages have cautioned us against unbridled greed. Those who see material items as the primary means of reaching happiness and meaning are on one of the most empty paths imaginable.

Only recently did I decide to refer to this addiction to the possesion of material objects as an actual addiction. I originally intended to write about "spending addictions." Then it became obvious that we weren't addicted to the spending alone. We are addicted to the fix value of the things purchased. We believe we need our trinkets in order to be happy, just as alcoholics believe they need alcohol, and food addicts believe they need their excessive food. Food addicts compulsively overeat and materialism addicts compulsively overbuy.

If we classify this addiction as only a spending addiction, then we will maintain the denial of those who also have work addictions in combination with the materialism addiction and who do not have to borrow money in order to keep up their material fixes.

Heroin addicts lie, steal, prostitute themselves, sell drugs, and rob others in order to get the money to buy their heroin. One can say the same of cocaine addicts. They even develop a secondary addiction to the gambling nature of the lifestyle they must lead to preserve their addictions.

Like heroin and cocaine addicts, materialism addicts lie to themselves about denying the needs of their families with the hours they work to acquire their objects of desire, and about being able to pay off credit card limits. Some of them prostitute themselves in marriages for money, push themselves and their spouses to overwork, and end up stealing from others by the legal means of bankruptcy in order to preserve their fixes. They also develop a secondary addiction to the gambling nature of their addictive spending, while the trinkets are the primary fix.

This addiction has the largest and best financed pusher network in the world. Advertisers bombard everyone with pitches for both the trinkets and the credit cards to buy them. People with this addiction push their parents, spouses, partners, and others who are potential sources of income to come through with the means of supplying this addiction. Children learn the addiction when parents buy them everything they don't need in the name of, or in the place of, love. Materialism addicts create excess stress for themselves and others in their lives so they can pursue what they simply do not need.

This addiction will be the most difficult to change at a societal level. Our culture is a far way from the levels and types of production which provide a measurably better standard for all. Our current tendency is to produce that which creates the most intense feelings of security, sensation, and power. We buy for the effect, not for the need. A societal belief in "capitalism," which is closer to a religion than to a simple economic strategy, underlies this pattern.

The Void, or existential vacuum, is dominant in this addiction. This society tries to make up for lack of true meaning with what Frankl calls the "will to money." The symptoms of addiction are most prevalent in this worship of materialism. There is a challenge ahead to overcome, individually and collectively, this slavery.

*Exercise Addiction.* We have been given bodies as "temples" within which we can live. The need for exercise and nutritional balance as a means of keeping up those temples is healthy. When we become so focused on our bodies and their beauty that we behave in self-centered and unhealthy ways, we are impairing the health of the temple we claim to be improving. We also spend so much time on the temple that we fail to put this gift to enough loving use.

The rise of exercise as a "good" addiction in our society has been rapid. Everyone advocates staying in shape and getting healthy. This requires a level of exercise. In the past few years, however, we have seen exercise evolve as a major societal expression of addictive core beliefs. We take the same feelings of fear of not being good enough, that underlie other addictions, and encourage each other to become involved with ourselves in a totally self-focused search for physical happiness and meaning.

There are runner's highs, steroid use, needless injuries, divorces, and other side-effects of plugging exercise into our symptom-treating model of addictive coping. We see some people who have constant injuries, malnutrition, and lack of resistance to disease because of their need to run many miles or race in triathlons.

Professional body-building is infected with epidemic steroid abuse. Professional sports are known for the use of drugs to enhance performance. This is an addictive pattern linked with drug, alcohol, and sex addiction in new types of addictive complexes. We see exercise paired with anorexia and bulimia in gravely destructive patterns.

Exercise is beneficial, but one needs to continue to balance this pattern, realizing that even the healthiest of activities can become addictive when practiced to extremes.

*Addictive Worrying.* I decided to include worrying in this list of addictions after reading *When Society Becomes An Addict.* Wilson-Schaef lists it as a process addiction. As it has always been rampant in my family, I have always been sensitive to the controlling nature of a habit of worrying. It was surprising, however, to see it in a list of addictions. After reading her book, it became obvious to me it is an addiction for many people and is crucial as a controlling strategy in relationship addiction.

Worriers are acting as if they are God. They assume the outcome they desire is the correct outcome, but are sure the universe will conspire to cheat them out of their wish. They bully others into feeling guilty if those others fail to show concern for the worrier's worries. They also create all kinds of negative self-fulfilling prophecies in their exchanges with others, especially children. *Worry gives one the illusion of power to predict.* It also gives one control over those others who will agree to protect the worrier from his fears. It is an elegant addiction, but one with no redeeming traits. It is only included in the "good" list because most of us have been conned by worriers to see it that way.

In recent years, my clients have been taught to be ruthless in their resolve to be free from the threat of others' worries. It is amazing how depression can lift in a family once the worrier is no longer allowed to dominate the family mood.

Now that we have reviewed these "good" addictions, you can see that they are not always good. Pain can result from imbalance in one's coping style, even when the focus of the addiction is perfectly acceptable to society.

## The "Bad" Addictions

The addictions in this list are less debatable and much more recognized by society. These addictions are to alcohol, nicotine, drugs, food, sex, gambling, and violence. The first four addictions are "bad" substance addictions, and the last are "bad" process addictions. In these addictive behaviors, it is easy to see negative outcomes, and those outcomes are being validated in research daily.

The following four addictions are the most recognized by our society as being destructive addictions. We agree to some degree that they are problems, and, though some of us practice one or more of these addictions, we usually describe them as problems.

*Alcohol Addiction.* Alcohol addiction and alcoholism is the most recognized addiction, in that it produces the most overt personal damage and familial damage to the most people in society, although it is not the cause of the most fatalities. Alcoholics Anonymous is the most famous of the self-help groups for addictions, and the one most widely used as a model for other self-help organizations. We now recognize that children of alcoholics, of all ages, have some unique problems simply as the result of having grown up in an alcoholic home. Health coverage for this disease is increasing among insurance carriers and there has been great progress in both genetic and behavioral research on this addiction in the last fifteen years. Still, the incidence of this fatal disease remains high.

One of the ironies of alcohol addiction is that the use of alcohol has no survival value whatsoever, yet two-thirds of the adult members of our society drink to some degree. Our country is heavily invested in the use of alcohol and the alcohol industry is one of the nation's most powerful lobbying interests. We believe in alcohol use, and it has been difficult to accept that our national drinking pastime is a threat when one abuses this chemical, and it is often abused. We have a need to deny that the chemicals which we endorse either overtly or covertly can be so damaging.

This denial is obvious when recovering alcoholics are in contact with those who are invested in their own drinking and who try to get the alcoholic to "control" his drinking. Over the years, one of the hardest facts to get members of our society to accept has been that alcoholics can't return to controlled drinking. This idea threatens the sense of safety of anyone who drinks. This is a very socially prescribed addiction. We believe strongly in the right to drink. Some of us are painfully paying the price for this cultural value.

All the world's major health organizations agree that alcoholism is a disease. It seems to develop primarily in persons with a family history of the disease, and seems to result from drinking excessively while having a hereditary biochemical defect which does not allow the body to process alcohol normally. The behavioral disturbances caused by the disease produce predictable emotional and behavioral problems among the children of persons with the disease and among the spouses of such persons. This disease is usually fatal if not arrested. In order to arrest the disease, one must learn to stay abstinent from alcohol. In addition, he must learn other coping mechanisms to replace the role of alcohol in his life. If this does not occur, he will usually exhibit stress-related symptoms and be at constant risk for relapse.

There are several symptoms of alcoholism, the most important of which seems to be the loss of the ability to predict one's behavior once one begins drinking. The inability to predict how much will be consumed and how one will act after consumption is critical. Also important are memory losses called "blackouts" and evil behaviors when drunk, called "Jekyll-Hyde behaviors" after the famous story.

Father Joseph Martin has the best advice for those asking if they have alcoholism or any other addiction. He says, "Anything which causes problems is one." If alcohol is causing problems in your life, see someone to learn if you have this disease.

*Nicotine Addiction.* I list this addiction separately because of my concern with the way we minimize this addiction in our medical approaches. This addiction kills more people than alcoholism, yet it is not classified as a disease process. The nicotine addict endangers the health of every member of his family and those in his work environment. Our Surgeon General lists it as our number one health problem. Yet, because of the political realities of our country, it is not classified as a disease. It is a disorder, but not a disease.

This is also one of the most difficult addictions to recover from. Nicotine is very powerful, and the effect of this drug occurs instantly. Only about ten percent of those who drink alcohol on a regular basis will become addicted to it. Almost one hundred percent of those who smoke on a regular basis will become addicted. Every therapist has treated alcoholics who had quit drinking years earlier and who were unable to beat the nicotine addiction. Some of my most difficult work has been with families of those dying from lung cancer caused by smoking. Some of the family members themselves were trying to quit the same habit, with great difficulty.

We give great amounts of lip service to wanting to help nicotine addicts quit using, yet we offer a pitifully small range of clinical options to someone with this addiction. We give it little attention, even though over a quarter of a million people will die from the side-effect diseases of this addiction in any one year. This is approximately three times the number of people who will die due to alcohol abuse, yet we are making no efforts to have treatment for this addiction covered by insurance nor to develop rational continuums of care for these addicts. This addiction, too, is protected by a large lobbying effort, and enough of us use nicotine for societal denial to be a factor. None of this changes nicotine addiction's status as our number one health problem in the United States.

We can only hope for more success in the future in developing a more rational, loving response to those addicted to this chemical. In the meantime, I advise anyone with this addiction to seek help with it as early as possible. The longer we participate in this behavior the harder it seems to be to quit. I wish you success.

*Other Drug Addictions.* This is a broad category, including everything from prescription drug abuse to marijuana, to cocaine and even to heroin addiction. It is also a growing concern to our government and, although the numbers of people in the broad category are decreasing, the use of cocaine in various forms is increasing. This concern is justified, as long as persons addicted to these substances aren't made into scapegoats as a way of denying our other addictions.

Most drugs of abuse offer no positive value to the user. Except for the small amount of prescription drug abuse which starts for legitimate reasons, the only use for these chemicals is to produce desired feelings. This is at best a neutral value.

The two drugs which currently produce the most concern are marijuana and cocaine, especially cocaine in the cheap, powerful form of "crack." Both are the focus of government efforts to clean up drug abuse and are the basis of massive illegal economies in Third World countries which supply us.

Marijuana is our most used and abused illegal drug. It is very controversial in that many say it causes practically no damage to the user. Others point to studies which indicate potentials of brain and lung damage with regular use.

The only positive uses for this drug have been in treatment of some eye problems and for persons dying of cancer. Except for these purposes, one uses this drug only for pleasure. Concerning its addictive potential, our program has treated several persons with both alcohol and marijuana abuse problems who either took much longer to quit the marijuana, or were unable to quit this drug, even though they had quit drinking when they had obvious alcoholism problems.

Cocaine addiction is the most psychologically powerful chemical addiction, with the possible exceptions of heroin and nicotine. The dependency on cocaine and crack develops very rapidly, and differences between use levels and overdose levels are almost totally unpredictable. The federal concern over these drugs is justified and I encourage my readers to: Stay Away!

As for any of the rest of the drugs of abuse, the only recreational use of these chemicals must occur as the result of illegal behavior. It is impossible to predict the actual ingredients of any illegal drug, unless you are the manufacturer. Stay away from those drugs. Furthermore, stay away from any non-medical drug use, as it is only a false way to meaning.

It is becoming much easier to receive quality treatment for drug addiction provided the addict has some money to pay for it. The drug abuse treatment network has improved greatly over the last twenty years in its knowledge and in the skill levels of its practitioners. Unfortunately, however, funding for treatment of these disorders has been woefully inadequate. There are, at least, few powerful lobbies directly promoting this form of suicide.

*Food Addiction.* Food addiction is a universal problem in our society and causes or worsens other disorders such as heart disease, hypertension, diabetes, skeletal/muscular disorders, and other stress-related problems. There are many societal pressures to eat unhealthy, high-calorie foods, and many people are overweight.

The mirror image of the problems of obesity, usually associated with food addiction, are the sister addictions of bulimia and anorexia. Many people go back and forth between these three expressions of out-of-control eating and do severe damage to their bodies.

Tendencies to overeat, like tendencies to overdrink alcohol, seem to have a genetic component. Studies show that the most important predisposing factor to developing obesity seems to be having overweight parents. We don't understand all the biochemical processes which cause some of us to crave food in greater amounts than we need, but we know that some of us are unfortunate in our choice of parents. This is a very complicated problem. The field of treating eating disorders is expanding rapidly and we are learning that many of our past assumptions about food addictive problems were simply wrong.

The person who is struggling with a food addiction may be someone who is extremely overweight, or someone who is practicing self-starvation, or someone in the middle who either is bulimic and purges excess food by vomiting or use of laxatives, or who simply eats more calories than are burned off.

The recovery from compulsive overeating in its three forms, obesity, anorexia, or bulimia, can be quite complicated and lengthy. We can, however, with proper diet and exercise, almost always overcome a problem with minor caloric imbalance. It simply takes effort. Sometimes the effort required seems devastating to the person who is already quite overweight, but the effort is worth making.

In those who develop bulimia and anorexia, the efforts to stay thin become misguided, compulsive, and unhealthy. There are definite differences between anorexia, or not eating at all, as a main power-fix, and bulimia, eating huge amounts of food and purging the food through vomiting or laxative abuse. Both, however, reflect an unhealthy obsession with physical definitions of self and are potentially fatal.

When food is eaten for emotional reasons, the potential for addiction is there. Few of us, however, do not enjoy eating. We will always have the ability to eat for both pleasure and subsistence. It is very important, therefore, to train ourselves to like those foods which are also healthy for us. This is the focus of any good plan to address food addiction. The better treatments also teach us to quit trying to maintain our emotional state by eating. Anyone who is either greatly overweight, starving themselves, or bingeing and purging needs to seek help with that disorder. Eating disorders are treatable, but it requires diligent effort to be successful.

Recent data shows a high incidence of major affective or mood disorders in sufferers of bulimia and anorexia. Persons who have this type of disorder correlated with a food addiction will require professional help. This is a very intricate phenomenon which we are just beginning to treat with consistent success.

## "Bad" Process Addictions

The following addictions are generally viewed as negative addictions and as severe problems in our society. I use the term "sex addiction" here to describe compulsive, fix-oriented sexuality. I think you will find some of this surprising.

*Sex Addiction*. The psychiatric literature has described patterns of addictive sexuality for years, with various explanations offered for them. They label it nymphomania in women; satyriasis, in men. Lately, some have labeled these patterns of disorders addictions. Dr. Patrick Carnes is a popular author and speaker on this subject. Carnes describes in great detail the addictive process wherein sex is the fix.

The sex addict substitutes a mood-altering experience for intimacy in his approaches to sexuality. Many of us have had sex with people we had known for short periods of time and for whom we primarily felt a sexual attraction. This is such common knowledge that a frequent way to refer to falling in love is to call it "falling in lust." This type of sex is potentially addictive. It is a very effective way of changing moods on a short term basis. And we are all exposed to media and other sources of sexual hype. When this type of sexuality becomes a major part of our coping strategies, we are misusing one of our most precious gifts.

When treating sex addicts, we see women who were married and have separated so that they can have four or more sexual encounters per day and hide it from their husbands. We see men who coerce their wives into having sex with others and are then overwhelmed with fear of losing their wives to better lovers, and with guilt from the behavior itself. We also see child molesters, both men and women, although our society doesn't seem to mind women having sex with underage boys nearly as much as it minds men having sex with underage girls. The men are usually reported by others. The women, if reported at all, are more often reported by a therapist because the boys see the behavior as something they want.

Another common pattern parallels the anorexic food addict. There are some persons who are fix-oriented in their sexuality and who are so determined to avoid inappropriate sexuality that they sexually starve themselves and their spouses of any sexual activity. In this situation, the addict is operating at a power level, and usually hides behind some moral front. When we look closely, however, there may well be sexuality outside of the marriage which the addict uses as a release valve for his sexual tensions. This person denies sex to the person in his life with whom sexuality is appropriate and gives sexual favors on occasion to people with whom there is no emotional involvement. This sneaky sexuality parallels the sneaky drinking of the alcoholic. When and if the spouse discovers the extramarital activity, it is usually devastating.

One of the cornerstones of sexually addictive behavior is that it most often occurs with little or no emotional involvement. Intimate sexuality and addictive sexuality have completely different purposes. Sexually addictive behavior occurs compulsively, as a fix to maintain a desired internal feeling state. The objects of the addict's sexuality are just that, objects.

Sex addiction usually starts with trying to feel safe and secure and often progresses to the purpose of gaining sensations and power over others. There is always an element of gambling in this addiction. The nature of the gamble changes as the addiction progresses.

Not all non-intimate sexuality leads to a sexual addiction, any more than all drinking leads to alcoholism. Some of us are prone to use sex as a generalized coping response and this is addictive. In later chapters, I will identify how the frequency of behavior leads to addiction.

*Gambling Addiction.* Gambling addiction comes in many forms and often interacts with the other addictive substances and behaviors in the lives of many addicts. The stereotype of the person who becomes obsessed with gambling until he loses everything and even steals or borrows to keep playing the horses, cards, dice, or some other form of financial gambling is indeed gambling addiction, and is very unhealthy. Historically, these are the persons treated for this addiction. They are not, however, the only gambling addicts.

Gambling is a common facet of many distinct addictions. The sex addict who participates in illegal sexuality may be as excited by the gambling involved as by the sexuality itself, whether the addictive behavior is patronizing prostitutes, pedophilia, or violent rape. The alcoholic who consistently drinks and drives in spite of previous problems is also gambling for pleasure when he continues to risk prosecution. The relationship addict who is keeping two or more relationships going at once is gambling, and this adds to the thrill. Relationship addicts usually choose someone who is in some sense a gamble. The drug addict is consistently gambling in his criminal behavior in using and procuring the drug. He may also be committing crimes to get the money to buy his supply. Criminals of all types gamble addictively when they continue to commit crimes for which they know they will likely get caught. The thrill of trying to get by with one more job has the same attraction as betting on one more horse.

As we continue to explore the gambling addiction, we will find that it is much more widespread than previously believed. It may be a cornerstone of the addictive process itself. Treatment centers for this addiction are not yet widespread. This will change as more of us become involved in state lotteries and other forms of gambling which have become the trend in recent years.

*Violence Addiction.* This category of addictive behavior is rarely described as an addiction. It is, however, addiction in its most severe form. This is a process addiction, in that specific types of interactions occur over and over between the violence addict and his victims. It occurs frequently in combination with relationship addiction, but also takes many other forms. For that reason, violence is considered separately here. There are several types of violence addicts.

Violent rapists are, contrary to the opinions of some theorists, sex addicts who operate at the power level of addiction. They find violence sexually exciting! This also occurs to varying degrees with people who must experience sex from a sadistic or masochistic posture. The violence and sexuality become intertwined in these persons.

Serial murderers are addicted both to violence and to gambling. They enjoy the feelings of power involved when they destroy another human being. We are just beginning to understand the mind of these extremely destructive individuals.

Teenagers in gangs can become addicted to the violence involved in inter-gang rivalries and in sexuality with the other members. The violence addictions of teens can rapidly escalate to being out of control, as the most violent members of teenage gangs tend to be successful in bullying their way into leadership. Much like a teen in a group of teenage alcohol abusers must drink to be accepted, a teen in a violent gang must be violent to be a full member of the group.

Soldiers often become addicted to the violent intensity of war. These soldiers have trouble with civilization when they have to live with the rest of us. The same type of peer pressure that occurs with teenagers occurs with soldiers. The hangover phenomena from participation in this addiction for those have well-developed consciences is often *Post Traumatic Stress Disorder*. We see this disorder both in the transgressors and victims of extreme violence. Both the aggressor and the victim become sufferers as the result of the out-of-control violent act.

Spouse and child abusers are often addicted to the rush they feel when they let their anger run free and cause others to cringe and cry. This rapidly progressing addiction is one of our most destructive. It is much more widespread than we can document, and has been so for centuries.

The addictive process holds true for violent persons. To date, we have little success with many of these people in treatment. This is an area for extensive research and extreme caution in treatment. Violence addicts are usually quite capable of fooling most people, including themselves, into believing they are cured. Like the alcoholic who states he will never drink again, these addicts can be quite convincing. Like any addict, the person addicted to violence must deal with this addiction one day at a time. If he promises more than that, he is lying. There may be no internal awareness of lying but it is a lie just the same. We have all heard or seen stories of the violent person who convinced mental health experts of a cure, only to rape, injure, or kill again.

As you can see, the line between those addictions which are "harmful" or "bad" and those which aren't is a mythical line. The bottom line is that frequently using the addictive model of coping causes problems, no matter what the object of the addiction might be.

You now have an overview of those behaviors and substances which are addictive. This is not a complete list. Some of you can look at your lives and identify addictions not on this list. That is not important. You now have the patterns and can identify enough to wonder about yourself if you have addictions. I hope I have shaken your ability to enjoy your addictions without questioning yourself. If that has occurred, then this volume is a success.

I invite you to continue and explore, in the following chapters, the ways we develop and recover from addictions.

*For Your Personal Growth*

*Go to an open AA meeting (You can find Alcoholics Anonymous in the White Pages) and listen to the others there. Ask yourself, "What if I am like them?" Find a copy of their questionnaire and answer the questions.*

*Look in your medicine chest and ask yourself how many of the drugs there are for mood control. Are they really needed? Talk with your children about drugs.*

*Do you gamble? How? How much has it cost you this year?*

*Are you ashamed of some of your sexual behavior? Do others confront you about being oversexed?*

*Do you enjoy violence in any form? Do you especially enjoy being violent towards those who are defenseless against you?*

# ADDICTIVE BEHAVIOR
## and PROCESS

*The addictive process is an unhealthy and abnormal disease process, whose assumptions, beliefs, behaviors, and lack of spirituality lead to a process of nonliving that is basically death-oriented. This basic disease, from which spring the subdiseases of co-dependence and alcoholism, among others, is tacitly and openly supported by the society in which we live.*

- Anne Wilson-Schaef

After reviewing the addictive options people practice, it is clear that we all act in some of the fix-oriented ways described in the last chapter. It is not acting in these manners in and of itself, however, which is the problem. The problem is that many of us become involved in a coping pattern in which these coping options are the primary ones in their lives. When this happens, we are in an *addictive process.*

### A Coping Style and Philosophy

This addictive process is a lifelong coping style. At first, one includes several behaviors in the coping list. Anyone with an addiction has, or has had, several other addictive behaviors which make up the coping style. This coping style has predictable patterns and outcomes, and can be mapped quite simply. I will explore and map this process in the next few pages.

Any coping choice has results. An effective coping choice abolishes or reduces stressors in our lives or adds to the meaning in our lives in other ways. Addictive coping choices typically only massage our most primitive feelings of security, sensation, and power. In so doing, they create a by-product of confusion between those feelings and more mature ones.

There are four major ideas in defining how addictions develop and showing how they fit together in the lives of the addict and those around him:

*1. The first idea is that an addictive process includes all the addictive behaviors an addict has ever used.*

*2. The second is the notion of progressivity, the idea that addiction is a self-reinforcing coping choice, which we tend to use more and more often due to short-term results. This progression relentlessly advances from security-focused through sensation-focused to power-focused addiction.*

*3. The third is the concept of "focusing," the idea that, as addictions progress and take more of our energy to maintain, we use fewer different addictive behaviors and "focus" on those behaviors which we perceive as working most effectively for our own mood maintenance.*

*4. The fourth idea is that of an "Addictive Complex," the development of a stable grouping of addictive behaviors which the addict uses as a primary coping strategy. The addict uses these addictions, usually about three, to attempt to cope with all major stress.*

This chapter and the next will describe these concepts in depth. In this chapter, we will describe the first two ideas. The following chapter will describe the other two.

**Addictive Process Revisited**

The easiest way to begin exploring how addiction works is to describe the process that occurs when any single addictive coping option "progresses" into an addiction and then a "disease." The addictive process may happen in a person's life with a single addiction, or it may occur with the use of several addictive options. This chapter will explain how any single addictive behavior functions within an overall addictive process

Before that, however, I would like to give credit to others. Several authors have been addressing this issue of addictive process. Three who have greatly influenced my work are Lawrence Hatterer, M.D., Kenneth Keyes, and Anne Wilson-Schaef. The definition of an underlying addictive process has been an important step in our understanding of this phenomenon. My perspective has partially evolved out of exposure to theirs. Let's review their descriptions.

Hatterer defines addiction as a coping style which consists of responding to even slight amounts of pain with large doses of pleasure. He sees this process as being the same, regardless of the specific presenting addiction. He also states that the major addictions are to chemicals, work, sex, food, and gambling. He finds the same patterns in all these addictions.

On the other hand, Kenneth Keyes, in his *Handbook to Higher Consciousness*, defines addictions as "emotion-backed demands." He states that addicts believe that they can be happy by catering to their emotional wants. He also states that no one has ever achieved happiness in that way.

Anne Wilson-Schaef refers to addictive process as an underlying "generic disease process" which is central to the coping strategies of Western society. She defines the process on a wider basis than Hatterer, making relationships a central focus, but narrower than Keyes, who defines addictions as any "emotion-backed demands." The addictive process, in all their opinions, seems to be a lifelong pattern, in which a person learns to cope with the slightest amount of pain, even anticipated pain, by resorting to fixes which provide either the reality, or the illusion, of large amounts of pleasure. I agree with their conclusions and have added a few of my own.

I stated my opinion earlier that "Addictive Process" is a generalized coping style in which a person learns to habitually respond to reality by using fix-oriented behaviors to bring about desired feelings rather than by responding directly to life's moment-to-moment demands. I see this as an ongoing process, and find it useful to break the process down into five more-or-less distinct levels. The lines between these are arbitrary, and it would be equally possible to use fewer or more divisions.

## The Five Stages

Looking at addictive process in terms of five levels simply allows good understanding without being overly detailed. The process can be presented as follows:

*Stage 1*. Enhancement Behavior
   *Stage 2*. Addictive Behavior
      *Stage 3*. Regular Addictive Behavior
         *Stage 4*. Addiction
            *Stage 5*. Disease

There are five distinct stages, with each stage representing a more advanced problem than the previous one. The first level of addictive process is the original experimental or "Enhancement" behaviors. I described these in the first chapter, Addiction In Society, and stated that we usually learn to associate pleasure with a behavior in a positive setting. At first, one uses fix-oriented behavior to enhance or magnify pleasures which exist in the setting itself. A good example is the use of a feast to enhance the feelings at a family gathering.

The second level is "Addictive Behavior," in which one uses the behavior to cope with problems. In this behavior, the person responds to perceived problems and the emotional symptoms he feels. He treats the symptoms by resorting to ritualistic, fix-oriented behavior, rather than by solving the problem, or by admitting that there may be no solution and letting go of the tension.

As shown in "The Introduction," the behavior looks like this:

| Problem | Symptom | Treatment |
|---------|---------|-----------|
| *Strep Throat* | *Pain* | *Asprin* |
| *Bad Marriage* | *Anxiety* | *Valium* |

In both the above examples, the person can expect no change to occur in the problem itself. We know the strep infection will worsen with this strategy, and the marriage may do the same. Both options are risks with no payoff.

The third level is "Regular Addictive Behavior," where the addictive behavior occurs in many situations. The difference here is that one shows frequent enhancement or addictive behaviors, but hasn't reached a point where it is painful to think of quitting these behaviors. Problems may, however, be starting to result from the addictive behaviors.

For example, a person may be coping with the pain of a divorce by having several sexual partners to build up his self-esteem. As a result, he may catch a treatable form of venereal disease. In addition, he may often drink to counter feelings of sexual inhibition, and to avoid pain.

### Withdrawal Begins

The fourth level is "Addiction," at which point withdrawal symptoms are present. This state is marked by the beginning of "withdrawal symptoms." These symptoms are:

*1. In spite of the fact his objective judgement tells him that the behavior is destructive, he takes no effective steps to change.*

*2. He rationalizes the behavior by giving reasons for continuing it which have no basis in fact.*

*3. When he thinks about quitting the behavior, he feels dread, perhaps terror, and clings to it even harder.*

*4. When he takes steps to stop, he suffers acute withdrawal symptoms, including physical distress, that he can only relieve by resuming the behavior.*

*5. When the behavior stops, there is a short-term feeling of being lost, alone, and empty, usually followed by, or sometimes accompanied by, a feeling of liberation.*

If the person in the preceding example has reached this point, he will have these withdrawal symptoms when he is unable to have sex or drink. He may also develop a fixation upon one person and feel severe symptoms when that person doesn't want him. The fixes which produce these effects during abstinence are the ones which have progressed to the point of being "Addictions."

The fifth, and last stage is "Addictive Disease." In this stage of addictive process, there are two aspects added to the addiction phase. The first is that, at this level, there has been significant physical damage due to the addiction. The second aspect is that the person will probably suffer long-term, or "Post-Acute Withdrawal" symptoms.

The person in the preceding example, if he reaches this stage, may have permanent damage from repeated cases of venereal disease, liver damage from drinking, or severe depression from losing a lover. Recovery from each and all these symptoms will take a period of several months. In addition, new coping philosophies will be necessary before recovery will be stable.

All addictions are capable of causing or becoming diseases. We know about the physical damage caused by alcohol and drugs, as these are highly publicized. We are also aware of the most frequent physical damage of sex addiction, venereal disease. We are even more informed of the physical problems caused by obesity and smoking. Heart disease is not usually described as being the partial result of work addiction, though we know this by folk wisdom. Any addiction is a stressor to the addict's system; when the stress becomes severe, disease develops, in one, two, or perhaps many forms.

**Post-Acute Withdrawal**

In the description of disease, I referred to "Post-Acute Withdrawal" symptoms. Post-Acute Withdrawal is well-documented in the recent alcoholism literature, but not in other addictions. In withdrawal from addictions, there seems to be a period of approximately two weeks in which the addict experiences acute distress. This is true of nicotine, marijuana, alcohol, and other addictions. If the addiction isn't too severe, this is the main problem for the person who has reached the "addiction" level.

Once a person has reached the disease level of addiction, however, there are less-severe, but quite bleak withdrawal patterns lasting for months after the beginning of abstinence. These post-acute symptoms have a great deal to do with failure in recovery. In alcohol addiction, these symptoms generally last up to six months, and involve several neurological problems. We witness periodic returns of less severe withdrawal symptoms for several months in most disease-level persons.

Now we will review the complete addictive process, so that these stages become clear. As I stated in the first chapter, Addiction in Society, we learn the positive value of addictive behavior most often when we use such behavior to enhance feelings which are already positive.

Addiction can, and sometimes does, develop as the result of the frequent search for the enhanced experience. Many of my clients developed a problem with addiction by falling in with a group that liked to party and liked to enhance its parties with addictive behaviors on a constant basis. Experts have long identified "peer pressure" as the major force for adolescents starting on chemicals, and most of my chemically dependent clients began using when they were adolescents. Some of them escalated very rapidly to problematic addiction.

**The Process At Work**

The first three steps start with frequent partying, leading to frequent pleasure-seeking, leading in turn to ignoring responsibilities. The process looks like this:

**Partying--- > Pleasure-Seeking--- > Ignore Responsibilities**

This is a simple process, and the behavior works until ignored responsibilities add up and become problems. Then it looks like this:

**Partying--- > Pleasure-Seeking--- > Ignore Responsibilities---**

## ------ > Problems Develop

Now we have the potential beginning of a new cycle, the cycle of addictive self-treatment, or the "Addictive Behavior" described earlier.

Let us assume the person is now married, and the problem developed with a spouse who wanted some of the person's time. The person has two options. The first option is the non-addictive one:

| Problem | Symptom | Treatment |
|---|---|---|
| *Spouse wants more time* | *Tension* | *Reduce Party-ing* |

This pattern is occurring daily as men and women mature and decide that their families are more important than the pursuit of pleasure. The response focuses on solving the problem. Now let's look at the addictive pattern:

| Problem | Symptom | Treatment |
|---|---|---|
| *Spouse wants more time* | *Tension* | *Drink* |

Here, the response is to treat the tension and ignore the problem. This means the problem will probably worsen. This is how the whole addictive cycle appears now:

**Partying-- > Pleasure-Seeking-- > Ignore Responsibilities-- >**

**------ > Spouse Wants Time---- > Tension--- > Drink More**

At this point, he is into "Addictive Behavior," and is well on his way to the later stages of "Addictive Process." To show this, we will start back at the first problem and go from there:

| Problem | Symptom | Treatment |
|---|---|---|
| 1. Spouse wants time | Tension | Drink more |
| 2. Family needs $ | Anxiety | Work more |
| 3. Sexual tensions | Depression | Drink more |
| 4. Car breaks down | Anger | Drink more |

At this point, the person is probably into addiction. He is using addictive behavior to deal with all emotional situations. Continuing, we find:

| Problem | Symptom | Treatment |
|---|---|---|
| 5. Loss of spouse's love | Loneliness | Drinks more |
| 6. Divorce | Loneliness | Drinks more |
| 7. Alcoholism diagnosed | | |

The person now has reached the level of "Addictive Disease," and will suffer the problems inherent in that disease. We will see further problems:

| Problem | Symptom | Treatment |
|---|---|---|
| 7. Alcoholism | Withdrawal | Drinks more |
| 8. Child support | Tension | Drinks more |
| 9. New spouse wants attention | Tension | Drinks more |

| 10. Health problems | Anxiety/ Depression | Drinks more |

This behavior cycle will continue until he stops drinking and starts addressing the problems. The combined feelings from the problems and addictions add up to depression and emptiness which are the direct result of incompetent coping with problems. He irrationally chooses self-treatment behavior over behaving in a way which removes the source of pain. The symptom of pain, not the cause of pain, is the focus of coping. The problems also grow because he ignores them.

## One More Time

Let's review another example of this process, so that you can again see how the behavior leads to new problems and an ongoing process. Persons from families with dominant addictions begin earlier than usual with "Addictive Behavior." They may skip the enhancement phase entirely. One common pattern among those from such families evolves as follows:

| Problem | Symptom | Treatment |
|---|---|---|
| 1. Alcoholic family | Anxiety/ Depression | Drink |
| 2. Alcoholic family | Anger | Take drugs |
| 3. Alcoholic family | Loneliness | Marriage |
| 4. Alcoholic husband | Trapped feeling | Eat |
| 5. Financial problems | Anxiety | Eat |
| 6. Problem pregnancy | Fear | Eat |
| 7. Obesity | Self-disgust | Bulimia |
| 8. Bulimia | Self-disgust | Diet pills |
| 9. Obesity | Self-disgust | Diet pills |
| 10. Addictive Marriage | Failure feelings | Diet pills Eat Drink |

| 11. Drug Addiction | Major Depression | Depression treatment |
| 12. Drug Addiction | Withdrawls | Drug treatment |

In only the last example is this person coping in a healthy, non-addictive manner. In all the prior coping examples, she is using a strategy which can only make her feel better for a short while. None of the prior strategies addressed the actual problem. As she used these coping strategies, her problems worsened, and she moved through the addictive process from addictive behavior to regular addictive behavior, to addiction, to disease. This example shows how the continued use of fix-oriented behavior results in disease.

Three of her treatment choices later became addictions and addictive diseases. Obesity, or compulsive overeating and its mirror image, bulimia, are diseases, as is drug addiction. In order for her to recover, she will need to stop these addictions, and deal with the other problems in her life.

## Blind Incompetence

In all addiction, a person who is not hypnotized into believing in the same addiction can see where an addict is acting incompetently. Any nonalcoholic can see that putting large amounts of poison in one's body will slowly kill it. A nonalcoholic smoker can recognize the poisoning effect of alcohol, but can't face the poisoning effect of cigarettes. Thin people can recognize the health risks of fat people, and fat people see the problems of anorexics. We can all see the incompetence in the addictive control strategies of others, but we all blind ourselves, to some degree, to the incompetence in our own strategies.

Whether or not we can see our own difficulties does not change the fact that we are less than competent in any area of our lives which we approach addictively. If I spend my time drinking and ignoring my marriage, my marriage will fail. If I eat to excess in a pleasure-seeking manner and don't exercise to burn off the calories, I will become overweight, create problems with my love life, and increase my health risks. If I eat excessively and over-exercise to burn off the calories, I will become fatigued because my exercise will become work or an addiction, and I will break my commitments to those I love. My only sane option is to change the way I eat, and exercise moderately.

The way to identify the areas of incompetence in your life is to look for areas of coping which adopt the goal of changing your feelings instead of the goal of dealing with stressors directly. If you recognize this tendency in yourself, it means you are trying to control yourself when you should be dealing with external realities.

We are also thinking addictively when the pursuit of pleasure consistently overrides other goals. The attitude that I'd rather eat, drink, have sex, work, or participate in any other addictive behavior than cope effectively is a sign of one or more addictions. It also reveals that the addictions are more advanced than those of the person who merely wants to change his mood before doing what he needs to do. While pleasure-seeking as a coping style is not the only way to display addiction, it is a tell-tale sign. However, pleasure-*seeking* is all that occurs, because all addictive behaviors fail to provide pleasure after a period of time.

Like all coping styles in our maps of reality, the addictive coping style is resistant to feedback, because it is protected by the defenses present in us all. It seems, however, that the addict's search for certain feelings somehow makes him defend addiction with excessive vigor.

**What Addictive Process Is Not**

In preventing confusion, it is important to realize what addictive process is not:

*Addictive process is not* loving someone in an unconditional, healthy manner. In fact, a person cannot love and seek addictive fixes concurrently. Addiction is based on fear, and no one can feel fear and love simultaneously.

*Addictive process is not* taking care of your responsibilities each day, or even most days, so that you have time to enjoy loving relationships and recreation.

*Addictive process is not* making love with someone you genuinely care for and with whom you have a commitment.

*Addictive process is not* getting appropriate amounts of your self-esteem from your material things, or from your job status.

*Addictive process is not* eating healthy, balanced meals.

*Addictive process is not* exercising on a regular, moderate basis.

*Addictive process is not* learning from life how to be more effective at taking care of yourself and loving those close to you as you age and grow in wisdom.

*Addictive process is not* having fun and pleasure as ways of enhancing other positive behaviors.

Finally, *addictive process is not* living your life in a balanced, natural, loving manner.

Addictive process has nothing to do with the above things. It does, however, have to do with living your life as if you are the center of the universe and using everyone else to allow you to perpetuate that illusion. It has everything to do with believing you have a constant right to demand and expect to get what you want in life.

Addictive process is most easily identified when a person finds that most of his life is taken up in trying to assure that his emotional state is one of constant pleasure. This is, at best, an impossible task for life is difficult. At worst, this pleasure-seeking leads to more and more pain because pleasure is always seen as a value in itself, instead of an outcome of the practice of healthy values. The addictive approach simply doesn't work.

*For Your Personal Growth*

Find a comfortable place, and sit or lie in a comfortable position. Now continue the review of your life, and look for the fix-oriented coping patterns you use. Start with the ones taught as enhancements and continue to ones you use now for changing feelings. Do you find yourself using new addictive fixes? How about finding yourself switching fixes, but spending more time in trying to maintain feelings you like by using a fix? Once you have identified the patterns, project them into your future. What can you sense developing if you continue your present path?

# PROGRESSION

*The first time I decided I had a problem with weight and needed to change, I weighed one eighty-five. The second time, it was two hundred. Now, its two hundred-ten. If I don't deal with my addiction right this time, I know I'll weigh more next time around.*

- A client

In the previous chapter, I described how addiction develops, going from simple "enhancement" behaviors to addictive "disease." We refer to this phenomenon over time as "Progression." I will explain progression in this chapter.

The addictive process is always progressive, no matter what combinations of addictions may occur. Regular addictive coping will always result in movement through the addictive process from enhancement behavior to disease and, in some cases, death. Until a person ceases to cope with life in an addictive manner, his life and the side effects of the addictions will get worse. This will become more and more disruptive if the whole addictive process is not arrested.

We find this concept of "progression" in the mainstream literature on addiction. For years, people have shown that alcoholism has a very predictable course and we know the same about several other specific addictions. We can predict major aspects of an addict's life and be largely accurate simply based on the choice of addictions. We know precisely how one's life will get worse in certain areas unless addictive coping is abandoned.

There are three interacting causes of progression in most addictions. The first cause is related to the rigidity with which we form and defend our "maps" of reality. The second is the increased physical requirements for drugs and alcohol in chemical addictions, and food in food addictions. The third is the result of addictive coping. The primary focus of this book is on the first and third reasons. This is not to minimize the reality of the second.

In the addictive process, problems get worse because the person's strategy for making things better focuses on solving the problem of troubled feelings, instead of on solving the actual problems behind those feelings. As problems get worse, feelings become more painful. The addict sets out to fix those feelings rather than the problems. This behavior, as I pointed out earlier, seems rational within the addicted one's map or model of reality.

Once our maps of reality are solid we resist changing them. We maintain consistency by means of distortion, deletion, and generalization. Once we have adopted a core belief that happiness exists at a physical level and is achievable by direct action on our part, we will embark on a sincere, but misguided, pilgrimage in search of it.

This pilgrimage proceeds in the direction of searches for feelings of security, sensations, and power. Until this search creates great pain for us, we do not question our core beliefs. We may question the means we use to obtain our goal, but we will find it difficult to question the core goal itself. This means that addictive behavior will continue until the pain is so great that questioning the goal is the only rational choice we have. In the meantime, we begin to pay a physical price for our coping choices.

We often describe progression in physical terms, and some addictions have definite, direct, physical consequences. A person with one or more of those addictions is committing suicide in a slow but steady manner. Because of the poor stress-management abilities of addictive coping, there will also be indirect physical results. These indirect consequences show themselves in the forms of stress-related physical, emotional, and mental illnesses.

As we well know, the use of certain substances creates physical dependence. There is also psychological dependence caused by using these substances and other behaviors in a person's addictive coping. In substance addictions, there will be a progression involving increases or decreases in the amount of the addictive substance required to produce a desired effect. We know that there are physiological reasons for this progression.

When a person is using one of these substances in an addictive process, that substance will often appear to be the primary addiction. From a physical standpoint, it will probably be the primary addiction, but mentally, it may merely be one of several self-destructive options the person practices. We can't ignore those other addictions.

Another outcome of addictive process is that our actual problems worsen as we spend more time in addictive coping rather than in reality-based coping. Our marriage problems get worse as we spend more time working. Our finances worsen as we spend more money drinking. Moreover, our self-esteem goes down as we see ourselves being less and less successful and competent.

The irony of addiction is that *the addict suffers progressive pain precisely because of the constant pursuit of pleasure*. At more advanced levels, he also feels less power over his life because of his constant attempts to feel powerful. There are several areas in which one experiences this progressive pain. He endures physical, emotional, mental, spiritual, and social/interpersonal consequences which progressively worsen. Coping options limit themselves, as the addict does the same incompetent things over and over again, becoming even less capable with age. The self-centeredness of the addictive style causes others to lose interest, and he is often alone, or with people with whom he would rather not socialize.

Eventually, the addict puts more and more time into the addictions and believes he is doing so rationally. Logic becomes the servant of, and slave to, the struggle to produce good feelings.

**From Security to Sensation to Power**

Several years ago, in a book titled *Handbook To Higher Consciousness*, Ken Keyes stated that the illusions of power people pursued in addiction fell into these three major classifications: security, sensation, and power. His book convinced me this is a useful way of looking at addictions. People are usually looking for happiness in one or more of these areas when they practice addictions.

This is a good way to describe the changing purposes of addictive behavior as the process progresses. These three types of experience are all dimensions of the pleasure-search of addiction, and are the foundation for understanding the flow of addictive process. These dimensions also represent the direction of the progression of addictive process.

In the previous chapter, I outlined the *addictive process* with five distinct stages. These stages are as follows:

**Enhancement Behavior-->Addictive Behavior-->**

**-->Regular Addictive Behavior-->Addiction-->**

**-->Disease**

As shown, the flow of the addictive process goes from enhancement behaviors, through the other stages, to disease. As this occurs, the purposes of addictive behavior also change in a predictable direction. Early addictive behavior will have the purposes of enhancing feelings of security and various pleasurable sensations. Later addictive behavior will have the purpose of producing feelings of power or control over self or others.

Some addictions start at the power level, and only progress in the magnitude of power sought. This is also important to know, because those addictions are usually quite dangerous. Pedophilia, for example, often starts at a power level. Relationship addictions for persons with painful family histories or mental instabilities may start at a power dimension and only progress in the degree and nature of power sought, including the degree and nature of violence present.

While people sometimes start out at the power-oriented level, most of us progress from security to sensation to power-based fixes. The progression from security to sensation to power is, therefore, the usual direction of the addictive progression. So we can add to the diagram of addictive process as follows:

**Enhancement Behavior->Addictive Behavior->Regular**

**Addictive Behavior->Addiction->Disease**

**Security------>Sensations----->Power-Control/Powerlessness**

So we see that as the addictive process progresses, the person shifts from security-seeking to sensation-seeking to power/powerlessness-seeking in his addictive behavior. Furthermore, as each addiction progresses, the movement is toward power-level addiction. Finally, as groups of addictions focus, the combined addictions move toward power-level outcomes.

Security, sensation, and power are all goals that animals have in their quest for physical survival. Any animal, including humans, needs food and shelter to survive. Only humans, however, can believe that a Mercedes is necessary for that survival. After any animal has enough food and shelter, it begins to search for sensation, such as more food and sex. Only humans search for cocaine.

After the animal has adequate amounts of sensation, it will focus on territorial, or power issues, and assure that it has adequate territory for survival. If it is a social animal, it may also try to be a leader. Only humans aspire to own everyone's living space and to rule them as well.

In one of nature's bizarre twists, once some animals decide there is no hope for survival, they will actually take a stance of determined powerlessness towards their environment. Beached whales, for example, will often refuse to go back to the ocean after they are put back in the water. Many animals will waste away and die when forced to live in the environment of a zoo. Humans have the same pattern.

Viktor Frankl in his classic, *Man's Search For Meaning*, describes how some of his fellow prisoners in World War II prisoner-of-war camps would do the same thing. Some of the prisoners, after so much abuse, would simply lie on their beds and die. They would smoke all their cigarettes, lie in their own excrement and fade away. Some addicts, such as the alcoholic, Howard, described in an earlier chapter, will do the same thing after so many years of abusing themselves by their own coping patterns and disease(s).

The pattern which evolves is that humanity has the ability, because of its superior brain development, to distort natural needs and create great confusion and damage for itself. We do not operate on instinct alone, and our massive brains use their logic capabilities to confuse our instincts.

Also, we take a normal survival tendency and magnify it into a search for happiness and meaning. This process is probably responsible for some of those achievements we consider man's greatest, and for much of our pain, including the pain of addiction.

### Assessing Progression

Security, sensation, and power are also dimensions of physical experience. We can benefit from knowing in which of these dimensions an addict is most involved in at any time. In general, the dimensions fall within a hierarchy, with security addictions being less self-destructive than sensation and power addictions.

The more all three of these dimensions are, or have been, present in any addict's addiction(s), the farther his addictive process has progressed. During the enhancement and addictive behavior stages, the person is primarily seeking security and sensations. Once regular addictive behavior develops, he is seeking both sensations and power over himself. As the frequency increases, the sensations become less fulfilling and he begins to explore the outcome of power over himself and others. Another way to say this is that since all addiction is the result of the pursuit of power over self and others, the more obviously an addict pursues power, the more advanced the addictive process.

As addiction develops, the power dimensions will come more and more into play. Finally, during the disease stage, this power dimension begins to present itself in a mirror-image pattern of powerlessness. This is the last and most critical stage for the addict. Let's explore how this works.

In much the same way that a child will manipulate for negative attention if no positive attention is available, the late stage disease-level addict will focus his efforts on achieving powerlessness. Once he is too sick to manipulate for power, and has given up on his abilities to cope successfully, he will use his manipulative resources to maintain the illusion of being guilt-free. He will also lead those around him to participate in this illusion. This is still a way of operating within the power dimension; it is just a specialized use of deletion, distortion, and generalization to protect an obviously flawed map of reality. At this stage, he will vigorously resist any descriptions of his ability to change things, choosing to play the constant victim or cripple. Now let's compare people functioning at these different levels.

An alcoholic who primarily drinks with friends and drinks for the high, but who does not bully his family, has not progressed as far as the one who enjoys being powerful and abusive when he drinks. The second alcoholic hasn't progressed as far as the alcoholic who is abusing his family when he is drunk or sober.

The work addict who gets most of his enjoyment from controlling his subordinates has a more severe addiction than one who enjoys the security of his job or the sensation of working. He will also be less serene because of the progression of his addiction.

Another comparison is the sex addict who simply wants feelings of security and sensation, versus the one who can't enjoy his addiction unless he is the giver or receiver of sadomasochistic violence. The masochist is practicing the powerlessness we described above and combining this with a means of producing intense sensations.

Finally, there is the cigarette addict who has tried several times to quit and faces early lung cancer. His doctor tells him that he must quit, but he believes at a subconscious level that he can't do so. His coping choice is to give up and take a stance that he is simply going to die. In taking this stance of powerlessness, he is able to upset his loved ones and spend his last days in intense, addictive relationships with them.

## This Is Normal

These addictive dimensions are in everyone. For example, we learn to manipulate for security at a very young age, and hang on to some of our childish behavior far beyond the time when it is useful. Expecting to be made secure is normal for a child.

In an adult, it is also normal to have some needs for reassurance about our security. We are all mortals, and the fact of impending death is enough to keep many of us looking for the illusion of security. Jealousy and fear of losing part of the trappings of our status are normal. They are, however, unpleasant and rarely necessary to experience.

Sensation addictions are less normal. While many of us are pleasure-seekers, few of us are so involved with the pursuit of sensation that we use this strategy as the core of our coping strategy. This is changing, however, and it will be interesting to see what percentage of our children are primarily sensation-seekers. There are some indications in research that the next generation may be more addictive than we are.

Severe power addictions are even less prevalent. While most of us enjoy the feeling that we are powerful, only a few are so involved in this addiction that the pursuit of power is the major focus of their lives. Most do, however, have relationships in which we attempt to manipulate and use power to the detriment of intimacy. Even this can be identified and changed.

### Hangover Phenomena

No matter what addictions a person chooses, progression will occur. He will also experience increased "hangover phenomena" in the form of physical, emotional, and spiritual pain as he becomes more dependent on addictive coping. There will also be less healthy love in the addict's life as the addictions progress through the dimensions we have covered. As we move towards the power/powerlessness experience of addiction, the pain we experience increases drastically. This occurs because loving behaviors and addictive behaviors are incompatible, and compete with each other for a person's time.

We all know about hangovers which occur when a person abuses alcohol. This painful condition is the focus of many jokes, and it is a price all drinkers pay eventually. We may not know, however, about hangover phenomena from other addictions.

The work addict who neglects the emotional needs of his family, while feeding his materialism and compulsive spending habits, will also experience hangover phenomena in the forms of depression, excessive fatigue, and loneliness as he gradually loses the skill to assure that his emotional needs are met. If he decides to cope with these feelings with alcohol, alcoholism may develop. If he decides to quit working so much, his family may shake up his addictive relationships with them because he can no longer keep them satisfied within their own addictions.

The sex addict finds that it requires more bizarre activities to turn him on, and that his unloving sexuality creates problems with his love life at home, putting him under pressure from the possibility of disease and arrest. He may gradually become impotent. In extreme cases, such as in severe pedophilia, guilt can become severe enough to cause suicide.

The chemically dependent person finds that her body requires more of the chemical than it once did. She now uses, not to get high, but to stay normal, and avoid physical withdrawal. In addition, she experiences deterioration of her health. She hears that she will eventually die or go insane if she doesn't stop. She also gets in legal trouble, and finds that the only ones who like her are other chemically dependent people.

The relationship addict finds that the current relationship has lost its spark too, and begins looking for someone new with whom to have an affair. She may have the scars resulting from the constant degradation which occurs as two relationship addicts try to control one another, and blame each other for their unhappiness. As she gets older, this gets less satisfying, as she can't lie to herself about the other person as effectively any more, and feels she is seeing the rerun of an exceptionally boring movie.

The person with all the above addictions will experience most of the effects listed in each of the individual addictions, more interpersonal tension and more rapid psychological and physical deterioration.

So we see that following such an irrational coping style as addiction results in increased tension and the increased motivation to further pursue addictive behaviors. As this occurs, the addict becomes more committed to the addictive style, and uses it to cope with the problems the style has created. The addictive style itself is the main problem from this level of progression, until recovery.

As this commitment increases, the addict defends the addiction, blaming others for the stress he feels. Because of the need for consistency in his model of reality, he can't see that trying to feel better results in feeling worse. He ranks consistency and predictability over accuracy in his world model and becomes more insane when this behavior doesn't work.

Over time, addiction often becomes the central coping style, demanding more of the addictions to get even minimal effect. The incompetent nature of an addict's life creates more severe problems, including the inability to maintain intimate relationships. This is due to the priority assigned to maintaining the addictions. This leads to further isolation. This result continues until the addict, for whatever reason, begins to develop alternatives to the addictive coping style. This *progressive incompetency* occurs, regardless of the specific addictions a person pursues. It will occur at different rates with different people, but it always occurs.

I could go on, but it seems obvious to me that a person's life would become more painful as he relies on any single coping style to deal with all of life's tensions, especially if that coping style failed to address any of the causes of those tensions. Indeed, as the addictive coping style adjusts feelings and ignores reality, it is one of the most insane coping options a person can use. We can easily see the progressive nature of the addictive process itself, once we focus on that process rather than on each addiction in isolation.

The outcome of progression is unhappiness and neurosis on the mild end, and insanity, incarceration, and death, on the severe end. There are also other shorter term consequences, like loss of marriages, and depression. We need to remember these outcomes and be honest with ourselves and other addicts about the areas of our lives which we threaten by our addictive coping patterns.

This description of the progression of addiction as moving through the dimensions of security, sensation, and power can provide a wealth of data for us all. Perhaps you can use this way of looking at yourself and your own coping patterns. Ask others to help you. If this analysis is two-way, it can provide clues to problem areas in your life. It can also lead to gradual feelings of freedom as you change your coping patterns to ones which work consistently for you.

*For Your Personal Growth*

*Review the addictive behaviors, if any, which you have identified in yourself and ask whether the preferred outcome of these behaviors are feelings of security, sensations, and power.*

*Which of the behaviors are you convinced you need to feel safe, either by yourself or within a group? Which produce the "warm" feelings that you like?*

*Which of the behaviors result in production of intense feelings? Do you feel nervous about losing the pleasure involved if you were to stop one or more of the behaviors?*

*Which of the behaviors give you feelings of power or control over yourself and others? Which produce feelings of frustration and powerlessness? Do any of the behaviors have a sadistic aspect, such as physical or mental abuse?*

# FOCUSING

*The only things in my life are my work, my drinking buddies, and my wife, in that order. Now you want me to give up the first two?*

- A client

In a previous chapter, I referred to four major concepts in the development of addictive problems. The two preceding chapters covered the first two, the concepts of addictive process and progressivity. I also described these processes in terms of the outcomes of security, sensation, and power/powerlessness.

The third and fourth concepts are the subject of this and the following chapter. These two concepts, in combination, help us better understand how the specific addictions fit into a person's life, and how one person's addictions fit with the addictions of others. The concepts which provide this understanding are, "Focusing" and the "Addictive Complex." In keeping with the previous chapter, we will explore how security, sensation, and power function in relation to these concepts.

## The Focusing Process

Until the recent past, we have studied addictions as separate subjects, and usually credited the increased pain an addict suffered to the progression of one specific addiction. As this book is about addictive process, the questions must focus on the process, rather than any single addiction which is part of that process.

The new questions are, how does an addict develop specific groups of fixes and how does he choose his addictions? We also should look at the results of those choices. This will add to our ability to see patterns we may have previously missed.

During the course of the addict's life, addictions usually become "focused" in "complexes" of mutually reinforcing behaviors. This process of focusing occurs over time and reflects an automatic decision-making pattern in which the addict narrows his choices of addictive behaviors based on the intensity of emotional and physical responses to the substances or behaviors used. He focuses upon those fixes which provide the most intense experiences of security, sensation, and power/powerlessness. Along the way, he drops those fixes which provide little intensity for him in these areas.

Focusing also occurs because the progression of individual addictions requires that the person invest more energy in those addictions, leaving less energy available for the rest of the addictive coping options. Each intense behavior he chooses requires energy which he can no longer spend on less intense behaviors. It is both a matter of choice and the side-effects of choice, a shifting of priorities.

Focusing, therefore, is the process whereby an addict chooses fewer and fewer specific addictive behaviors to use in an addictive coping style. This narrowing of choices occurs throughout the course of the addictive process until he creates and attempts to maintain a precise, comfortable number of addictions.

Focusing occurs for physical and psychological reasons, in combination with the person's reaction to external social pressures. One chooses those fixes which seem to do the most to create security, sensation, and power-related feelings. As this occurs, fixes which no longer seem to be effective for mood control are dropped from the menu.

### The Restaurant of Life

Focusing is similar to our experience when dining at a new restaurant. When we first go to a new restaurant we review the menu carefully, selecting from the complete menu based on our prior experience with the foods. We make a choice, and we return to the restaurant if we liked the outcome. When we return a second time, we may try a new menu item. If this tastes good, we value the restaurant more highly. If we return for a third time, we may find even more items we like. Eventually, we will know which items on the menu produced the most pleasure, and will choose from among those items.

Once we are familiar with a restaurant, we begin reviewing a menu in our minds before we get there. We review our own mental copy of the menu before choosing our meal. This internal menu is the result of our focusing on those foods we liked in our previous visits to the restaurant. The result is a limited menu, with many of the other items forgotten for the moment.

An identical process occurs in our lives when we are choosing among addictive options. We generally focus our awareness in the same way described in the restaurant example. We will usually limit our mental menu to a small number of items in both situations. I find that I can recall two to four menu items in the restaurants I usually frequent. This is consistent with my clients' and my own addictive experience. In addiction, as in restaurants, *we will usually drop some addictive alternatives and keep others until we stabilize at about three options.*

Some people fail to focus at all, and retain the same fixes they had as teenagers. The result is an "Unfocused Addictive Complex." So whether or not focusing occurs is an important aspect of one's addictive patterns.

Understanding focusing allows us to better grasp how addictions develop in such diverse ways, and also lets us see why our attempts to explain it have been myopic. Focusing and the addictive complex are related phenomena, but the addictive complex can also exist in an unfocused manner. This is something which we have previously failed to recognize as addiction.

**The Addictive Complex**

An addictive complex is a mutually reinforcing, compatible group of addictive behaviors that an addict has found to be the most successful combination in helping maintain security, good feelings, and illusions of power and self-control. In the addictive complex there may be one addictive behavior which has progressed to an addiction. It will often be a socially acceptable addiction. The other addictive behaviors may have only progressed to the regular addictive behavior stage.

Usually, however, there will be or will have been at least three addictive coping patterns which have progressed to the stage of being legitimate addictions. This addictive complex often narrows or focuses over time, and usually achieves three or more addictions before the complex crumbles because of the development of addictive disease.

For example, alcoholics, until late progression, aren't usually just alcoholics. They are often work addicts, sex addicts, relationship addicts, food addicts, or gambling addicts. They regularly have multiple addictions which frustrate every person in their lives including those trying to help them change coping styles. Even if they are not practicing these addictions, they were once, and will want to again if they quit drinking. They will want to continue addiction with or without keeping drinking as their main fix.

In my experience, an addict's pain is more often related to the state of his complex of addictions than it is to the outcome of the progression of one specific addiction. When rapid progression occurs in one addiction, it is often a reaction to the pain created by an imbalance in the addict's addictive complex. Let's review an example of how this complex develops.

**How Focusing Works**

As stated earlier in this book, addictive behavior is normal. By the time we reach our teens, our culture has educated us about which behaviors we can use as fixes. We truly develop menus of pleasure producers in our heads. A teenage male, sitting around feeling bored, will consider a list that might look like this:

*DRUGS * SPORTS * ALCOHOL * WORK*
*FOOD * TV * SEX * FAST CARS*

He will often choose to alleviate his boredom with one or more of these menu items.

The same person, at age 21, may have a slightly different menu in mind. It might look like this:

*SEX * FOOD * ALCOHOL * WORK * SPORTS*

At age 27, this person is married. The menu now looks like this:

*RELATIONSHIP * FOOD * ALCOHOL * WORK*

A further focusing has occurred. His sexual pattern has changed because of the social pressure of the marriage contract.

At age 35, he gets arrested for drunk driving and is sent to me for evaluation to see if he needs treatment for drinking. His once elegant menu is down to three items:

*WORK * ALCOHOL * RELATIONSHIP*

He now has alcoholism and has formed a focused "addictive complex" of three counterbalancing addictions.

He works to maintain the drinking and the relationship. He drinks as a primary illusional source of pleasure (he hasn't truly enjoyed drinking for years), and he is in a love-hate relationship with his wife which also fails to provide real pleasure. She is jealous of his other addictions and very angry. All three of these options are addictions because the idea of quitting any one of the three produces emotional withdrawal symptoms.

This is typical of the 35 year-old alcoholic entering treatment. This pattern of three addictions is usual at this age, and works psychologically like a three-legged stool. When he gets below three options, he feels out of balance. If he doesn't quit drinking at age 35, he may come back in at 40 with his third DWI and this menu:

*ALCOHOL * WORK*

His wife became fed up with his incompetence and left. At this stage, the addict becomes extremely uncomfortable. This pattern of two addictions is not enough, and he will attempt to start a new addictive relationship to give him a minimum of three addictions and restore his feeling of balance. In the meantime, he will probably drink more, overeat, or binge on sexual relationships until he finds another addictive relationship.

At any point in this process, he had an addictive complex. He had groups of addictive behaviors, which allowed him to manipulate his feelings from the beginning. He dropped some of the behaviors due to reasons of practicality and effectiveness. He stabilized, like most of my clients, at three addictions until someone else upset his stability and plunged him into pain which could not be effectively treated with only two addictive options.

The thirty-five-year old's three addiction pattern is the most common focused addictive complex I observe. At sixteen, he had several fixes for coping options. At this stage, he was practicing addiction in an unfocused manner, and thus had an "unfocused addictive complex." This later changed.

The concept of an "Addictive Complex" is crucial in understanding how such an inept coping style as addiction can have cohesion and continuity in the face of increased pressure and incompetence. It also allows us to know, in the *unfocused addictive complex*, that the coping style of addiction can occur, complete with progression and death, without the person ever being identified as having addictions, even by an addictions worker.

### The Unfocused Complex

An *unfocused addictive complex* is one in which the complex begins at a young age, with the person using several fixes to cope with life. In this complex, however, the addict keeps most or all the original addictive behaviors in the coping strategy, and tries to do them all. This person is an "unfocused addict." This type of addict has no fewer problems than focused addicts, but is harder to identify as an addict unless one knows this pattern.

Just as alcoholics have been misdiagnosed for years, unfocused addicts are underdiagnosed by their health professionals and loved ones alike. First, however, it was necessary to show focused addictive complexes in order to understand its opposite.

Let's look at another example. At age 16, Tony, one of my clients, had this list of fixes:

*FOOD * SEX * SPEEDING * SPORTS
HUNTING * RELATIONSHIP (MOTHER)*

He felt comfortable, except for mom and her overprotection.
At age 20, he had this list:

*FOOD * SEX * ALCOHOL * HUNTING *
RELATIONSHIP (WIFE)*

He had just started drinking, and liked it. He had a new marriage, but was also having sex with several women, including his uncle's wife. His uncle had forced Tony to commit fellatio on him several times during my client's teens and he was getting even.

When Tony was 30, his list looked like this:

*SEX * HUNTING * DRINKING * MARIJUANA
RELATIONSHIP (SECOND WIFE)*

He had remarried, and was very dependent on alcohol and marijuana. He was also having sex with other women when given the opportunity.

At age 36, when I met him, this was his list:

*RELATIONSHIP (GIRL-FRIEND) * MARIJUANA*

He had rather rapidly gone from five addictive options to two. He had quit drinking because of almost overdosing, and had quit hunting because of the time his other addictions were taking. He had decided to stay away from casual sex because of concern over his inability to commit to one person. He was very depressed at the time, largely due to withdrawal symptoms from his addictions. He was still trying to focus on changing his feelings rather than his problems, and he was not being successful. He still couldn't understand that his addictions were part of a process which he had not begun to address.

The above pattern had no stability. Within a few months, he smoked marijuana, got drunk after he was high, and molested his nine-year-old daughter. He returned to all his previous damaging addictions, and added a new dimension to his sex addiction within two days. At this point he became very depressed, and began to try to learn to live non-addictively. He quit smoking marijuana, drinking alcohol, and left his girlfriend. He has had one alcohol relapse since then. He is again involved in an addictive relationship, but he knows it, and is reviewing his involvement.

At age twenty, Tony had an unfocused addictive complex, and was a candidate for treatment. The combination of his preference for alcohol and sexual behavior were clues that he was already a firm believer in addictive coping. All his addictions became worse for the next ten years before he began focusing his addictions.

At age twenty-five, he had attempted suicide because of the depressive hangover phenomena from his combined addictions, but the psychiatrist treating him missed his addictions and diagnosed simple depression. For ten years, he was an unfocused addict who had periodic contact with mental health professionals, but he was diagnosed alternately as depressive and as having a passive-aggressive personality disorder. He feels less depressed now and uses little passive-aggressive behavior in his relationships.

Tony eventually focused his addictions, but not everyone does. We see unfocused addicts everyday and fail to recognize them. Persons with high needs for control, who work, drink, have sex, promote themselves, exercise, achieve addictively, and have addictive marriages and families are unfocused addicts.

They are often called "type A personalities." They die of heart attacks and have been a concern to heart specialists for several years now. They are taught to relax their needs for control, and it works in several cases. They often die of "stress-related" disease.

**Addiction Is A Stressor**

Addictive coping is, in and of itself, a constant stressor. Besides a stable culture, Antonovsky lists, in *Health, Stress, and Coping*, several "resistance resources" to stress and tension, and states that the lack of one of these resources is a constant stressor. The more of these resistance resources we lack, the more constant tension we experience. One of those resources, for example, is a "rational, flexible, and farsighted" coping strategy. We need to realize that addictive coping is the direct opposite of that resistance resource. In addition, it can destroy other resources over the course of its existence.

An addictive complex allows us to feel we are coping effectively when we are not. The more addictions we have in our complex, the more we are unable to recognize our incompetence, because the complex's main function is to distract us from knowing that we are not coping well. Denial becomes much more painful and difficult to maintain when the number of addictions in an addictive complex drops below three. Perhaps this is because we need more than two options for adequate distraction. This creates much stress.

**Time and Addictive Complexes**

One of the important things about the addictive complex is that it allows us to judge the progression of our combined addictions, by assessing the percentage of time we spend using one or more of them. The more time a person spends using one or more of the fixes in the complex to cope, the further the addictive process has progressed. We need to look at the combined addictions to assess this fact, because looking at only one addiction can mislead us.

In diagnosing alcoholism, for example, I ask the client how much of his time during the day he structures either drinking, thinking about drinking, or recovering from the last drinking episode. Often, a person admits that upwards of eighty to ninety percent of his time is taken up in thinking about this addiction. In assessing the addictive complex, I ask how the rest of his mental and physical time is spent. Usually, the combinations of addictive options in the complex will take up almost one hundred percent of his time. This pattern is consistent with all the addictions I see. There will be one addiction which structures most of the client's time, combined with two or more addictive options which consume virtually all physical and mental efforts.

In the first example in the chapter, looking only at the alcoholism would give us a fair idea of his progression, allowing us to make some accurate predictions about his future behaviors. In Tony's case, however, failure to look at the addictive complex, and looking only at his alcohol and drug addictions, would not have allowed us to see that his other addictions were likely to cause problems for some time to come, regardless of his not drinking. Not drinking, for Tony, only represents a focusing of his addictive complex, not freedom from his addictions.

Identifying someone with an elaborate addictive complex as primarily an alcoholic, drug addict, or personality disorder, while ignoring the other addictions in the complex, is both less successful than desired, and uncomfortable for the addict. The whole complex of addictions needs to be identified and addressed to prevent surprises and failures. This is simple and easy to do, once we know to look for other patterns.

We can also change ourselves more easily when we know the range of fixes we use to handicap ourselves. Knowing the amount of time we spend in our addictive patterns is crucial to beginning our own recovery.

In order that you have a clear understanding of focusing, I will review an example used in Addictive Behavior and Process. The example is the one of the daughter of an alcoholic:

| Problem | Symptom | Treatment |
| --- | --- | --- |
| *Alcoholic family* | *Anxiety/ Depression* | *Drink* |
| *Alcoholic family* | *Anger* | *Take drugs* |
| *Alcoholic family* | *Loneliness* | *Marriage* |
| *Alcoholic husband* | *Trapped feeling* | *Eat* |

| | | |
|---|---|---|
| *Financial problems* | *Anxiety* | *Eat* |
| *Problem pregnancy* | *Fear* | *Eat* |
| *Obesity* | *Self-disgust* | *Bulimia* |
| *Bulimia* | *Self-disgust* | *Diet pills* |
| *Obesity* | *Self-disgust* | *Diet pills* |
| *Addictive Marriage* | *Failure feelings* | *Diet pills* |
| | | *Eat* |
| | | *Drink* |
| *Drug Addiction* | *Major Depression* | *Depression treatment* |
| *Drug Addiction* | *Withdrawals* | *Drug treatment* |

This person started out with few addictive options. Drinking, eating, and relationships were the elements of a focused addictive pattern early in her life. Once she started the diet pills, she had focused on chemicals, eating, and the bad marriage as her addictive complex. She stayed very unhappy within that pattern. I can make some predictions about this person in recovery.

At the time of entering treatment, this was her coping pattern:

| Problem | Symptom | Treatment |
|---|---|---|
| *Obesity* | *Self-disgust* | *Diet pills* |
| *Addictive Marriage* | *Failure feelings* | *Diet pills* |
| | | *Eat* |
| | | *Drink* |
| *Drug Addiction* | *Withdrawals* | *Drug treatment* |

You will notice that she has three addictions; food, relationships, and drugs. During the drug treatment, she will be attempting to quit her drug use. This will result in urges to compensate by increasing the addictive interaction with her husband, or by increased eating.

One of the impulses of someone with this pattern is to begin an affair with another client of the treatment center, an addictive relationship which serves to treat the pain of withdrawal for both of them. If this occurs, her pattern will look like this:

| Problem | Symptom | Treatment |
|---------|---------|-----------|
| *Addictive Marriage* | *Failure Feelings* | *Diet pills*<br>*Eat*<br>*Drink* |
| *Drug Addiction* | *Major Depression* | *Depression treatment* |
| *Drug Addiction*<br>*Affair* | *Withdrawals*<br>*Guilt* | *Abstinence*<br>*Eat*<br>*Sex*<br>*Fights with husband* |

She will attempt to maintain three active addictions, and she will have done so with the affair. If she is able to process all her addictions with the staff and begin a self-help program, she can break out of this pattern. It does, however, require hard work.

### Variable Addictive Complexes

The previous example was one of a person with a three-addiction addictive complex. Even though she had three interrelated addictions, her addictions had progressed to different levels of the security, sensation, and power continuum during the focusing process. Her marriage, drug, and eating addictions had progressed to the powerlessness level, but the new affair would most likely begin at the security and sensation levels, then rapidly catch up with the other two. We know, however, that this lady will have severe post-acute withdrawals because she has more than one disease-level addiction. Her recovery will take work and require intensive support.

One can consider each addiction separately and jointly as I did in this example. In this way, we can tell when a person has only one or more than one addiction which has progressed to being an addictive disease. This is important knowledge, whether I am looking at someone else, or at myself.

We will find ourselves at different places at different times with each of the addictions in our complex. Separate addictions in our complexes progress at different speeds, with each addiction pursuing one or more of the three major outcomes. We may work addictively with our concentration being on security, then pay prostitutes for sadomasochistic favors, and use cocaine purely to enhance sensation. If this is our pattern, we are likely to experience the most severe problems from our sex addiction until this pattern shifts. If the cocaine use becomes an addiction, it will probably cause us the most problems.

We can diagram such an addictive complex as follows:

| **Security** | **Sensation** | **Power** |
|---|---|---|
| *work* | *cocaine* | *sex* |

This gives us a way to list the addictions within a complex, map the changes as they occur, and predict changes based upon the beginnings of progression from security to sensation, or from sensation to power.

As people begin moving toward recovery, they need to look at these patterns and decide which addictive behaviors require abstinence, and which ones they can or must learn to practice in moderation. We will present the guidelines for making this decision in a later chapter.

If the normal pattern holds true, the pattern in the previous example will not remain stable for long as outlined. Cocaine rapidly becomes a power-level addiction, and we can expect the pattern to soon look like this:

| **Security** | **Sensation** | **Power** |
|---|---|---|
| *work* | *sex* | *cocaine* |

It is obvious that there is always a dynamic potential in any addictive pattern. Given enough data, we can make accurate predictions of the future of someone's addictive complex.

In another pattern, some addictions start at the power level, and only progress in the levels of power sought. This is also important to know, because those addictions are usually extremely dangerous. Pedophilia, for example, often starts at a power level. Relationship addictions for persons with traumatic family histories or mental instabilities may start at a power dimension and only progress in the degree and nature of power, including the degree and nature of violence present. Understanding these patterns is important as we attempt to define our problems accurately.

## Patterns of Change

Even though we will be at different places at different times with different fixes in our addictive pattern, we will gradually spend more and more of our time in our combined addictions until we find another way to cope. Some of our addictions will have to be completely abandoned. Others can be "upgraded," in Keyes' terminology, to preferences. There are several ideas which are relevant to the decision to abandon or upgrade an addiction.

People do move away from an addictive lifestyle. Depending on the addictive configuration, the addict will be able to slowly adopt less addictive coping, once the hangover phenomena overrides the ability to lie to himself about the behavior. Once this occurs, he has "hit bottom," and is ready to begin learning other coping means.

## Now We Understand

The addictive complex is one of the prime reasons an addicted person needs to participate in self-help groups. Treatment long enough to achieve the downfall of the addictive complex is impractical and too expensive. In addition, the recovering addict needs several examples to choose from in deciding which new patterns he wants in his life. Other successful people offer these examples.

The addictive complex can also help us understand how some people seem to have an "addictive personality." Such a personality has never been proven in research, but someone with several addictions would appear to have such a personality when quitting an addiction and compensating by going back to a previous option. *Rather than this being an "addictive personality," it is an habitual coping pattern.* It is a cognitive and behavioral map of coping, not a combination of inherent personality traits.

The discovery of the process of focusing and the addictive complex did a great deal for my understanding of addictions. Even more fascinating are the insights gained from studying the complexes of addicted persons involved with each other in marital and family relationships.

*For Your Personal Growth*

*Relax and review your life as it is now. How is your time structured? Do you find yourself doing few activities? If so, how does this compare to the expectations for your life you had as a younger person? Are the activities you identify listed in my list of addictive behaviors? How has the list changed since your early years? Consider this closely as you decide if your life is as meaningful as you had hoped, or as meaningful as you want it to be.*

# COMPLEMENTARY
# ADDICTIVE RELATIONSHIPS

*An alcoholic system - actually, any addictive system - is contagious, and those who live within it become infected with the disease sooner or later.*

- Anne Wilson-Schaef

In all the addictions writings, the interdependence of addicts and those persons close to addicts is discussed. The term "co-dependent" is most often used to describe a person who is closely involved with an addict. There is little writing, however, which reveals how the addictions in one member of a relationship relate to the addictions in the other member or members in that relationship.

I have already described the relationships between addicted persons as "relationship addictions" or "co-dependent relationships." I described how we use each other as objects to provide feelings of security, sensations, and power. Besides this relationship addictive pattern, there are other ingredients which glue addicted persons together.

Hatterer described the relationships between addicts as being ones in which they "complemented" each other in a symbiotic manner. He avoided the inherent assigning of responsibility involved in calling one person an "addict" and the other a "co-addict." This approach works for my clients and this success has inspired me to expand his thesis.

In my observation, primary relationship patterns exist between addictions, both within the identified addict, and between the addict and those close to him or her. One can assume until proven wrong, that the adult person involved in a painful close relationship with an addict maintains that relationship precisely because it reinforces the ability to deny addictions, and also provides excuses for participating in those addictions.

Patrick Carnes described this by saying that addictions come in "families." It is as if the addictions themselves are family members relating to one another at all times. They come into the family life, age, die, and are mourned until they are replaced by new members. Individuals may marry and divorce different addictions at different times, but they always remain part of the family tree.

This is different from the generally held view of co-dependency, which states that the significant other of an alcoholic, for example, suffers severe problems primarily because he is close to an alcoholic. While this is one of the reasons he has problems, such a person suffers the most difficulty because he has addictions of his own, and the relationship with the alcoholic is one of those addictions.

In my view, there are only "co-dependents" and victims. The adults in a family are the co-dependents and the children are the victims who are being trained to be co-dependents.

There are few of us who have no one to reinforce our addictions. The severely addicted person has a network of others who depend on his addictions in order to justify their own. Most situations are ones in which two or more addicted adults live together that they might be better able to practice their individual addictions. Any children in the environment become pawns in the inevitable addictive relationship patterns.

Some of the nonalcoholic persons we call "co-dependents" even seek out one alcoholic after another in order that they may keep from facing their own addictions. The co-dependent person who is alcoholic seeks a spouse with addictions of his or her own, which will distract the spouse from the alcoholism. In this way, they both can continue their individual addictions with no guilt about their addictive behavior. *Their relationship addictions allow them to deny the other addictions in their lives.*

If you are an adult living with another adult who is obviously an addict, you can assume that you are probably just as much an addict as that person. If you view yourself as a victim in the relationship, you can be even more sure that you are at least addicted to the relationship between the two of you. This is usually a good place to start recovery.

**Shared Addictive Complexes**

Persons involved with addicts with a certain number of addictions will usually be protecting the same number of addictions of their own. In this sense, one can say they share an addictive complex. This provides a balance until one or the other progresses to one less addiction. At that time, the relationship becomes unstable until someone reestablishes a balance of addictions.

This works much like a teeter-totter on a playground. Two people with identical weights can sit on one and balance it with no effort, but if one person were to suddenly discard one-third of the weight on his side, the other person would fall to the ground and the lighter person would be up in the air. Keeping the previous balance is difficult until the other person either drops the same amount of weight or until the original person regains the weight he had in the first place.

This balance often occurs in my marital sessions. The addict comes into my office for marital counseling. He is with his wife, also an addict. This is their pattern.

| **Husband** | **Wife** |
|---|---|
| *Work* | *Spending* |
| *Affair* | *Food* |
| *Relationship* | *Relationship* |

She is upset because he recently changed a pattern of periodic sexual encounters, which she could tolerate, to a sexual affair with someone more attractive than herself. He is upset because she has become so overweight that he can't find her attractive anymore, and he is also overloaded with the bills she has created with her compulsive spending. Each feels their own upset and addictions are the other's fault.

An interesting part of this pattern is that the wife has the morally superior position here, and most outside observers would feel that the husband has caused the current problem. The wife will usually negotiate for him to change addictions and try to keep hers intact. She will especially resist confrontation about her spending and eating, perhaps believing it is his job to keep her safe in her addictions. He will, likewise, resist giving up his work and sex addictions. Neither one of them will see the mutual attempts at manipulating each other as signs of a relationship addiction between them.

He may offer to give up his affair, if she gets thin and is able to cater to his sexual addiction, which may have been a reason for her focus on food in the first place. If the marriage is to change, all their addictive patterns will need to change, and they will have to learn to love each other, instead of constantly judging and trying to change each other.

The above example has no alcohol or drug addiction in it, but the dynamics are the same as in alcohol and drug affected situations. For example, the following is a common pattern in alcoholism cases.

### The Pressure Backfires

Doug is an alcoholic and Sarah, his wife, is a food addict. Their recovery began when Sarah pressured Doug into treatment because she couldn't live with his drinking any more. Doug went to a treatment center for "evaluation," and Sarah put his suitcase in the trunk without his knowing it. Once he was there, he was pressured into a thirty-day treatment program, and Sarah agreed to participate in the week-long family program. Later, in her talks with me, she explained how she had felt justified, because "someone finally was getting to him about his problem!"

Her later experience was far from pleasant. Once she started the family program, he confronted her about being five-foot-two, and weighing two hundred pounds. She countered about how it feels to make love with someone who always smells like a brewery. Suddenly, she was being confronted about her own problems, and she became very defensive. When treatment personnel recommended that she attend Al-Anon, for the spouses of alcoholics, and Overeaters Anonymous for her addictive eating, she became very angry. He had the problem, not her. In actuality, their pre-treatment complexes looked like this:

| DOUG | SARAH |
|------|-------|
| *Alcohol* | *Food* |
| *Work* | *Work* |
| *Relationship* | *Relationship* |

Sarah had taken up a job a few years ago, and it had consumed most of her life. Before that, she had three affairs, which she blamed on her husband, and spent most of her time addictively controlling her children. She forced Doug into treatment primarily because his alcoholism was making him so sick that he couldn't work regularly, and was about to lose his job. This threatened her certainty that she could continue to have all the food and other things she wanted.

She had pressured Doug into treatment because her addictive complex was threatened! Up until that time, she had been able to survive with the subtle advantage of playing victim with her friends for having to live with him.

My experience shows that the alcoholic has a better chance of recovering from his addictive patterns than does his wife. This happened with this couple when Sarah divorced Doug rather than commit to her own growth. He has since stayed sober and remarried. I recently saw her in public. Her food addiction is still active and her second husband is alcoholic.

There are many more alcoholics in Alcoholics Anonymous than there are "co-alcoholics" in Al-Anon, even though Al-Anon doesn't directly confront their other addictions. Seldom does someone tell the co-dependent that he or she is also an addict who simply has a different combination of addictions than the alcoholic.

In the literature on alcoholism, it is often said that the family members of an alcoholic are sicker than the alcoholic. While this is debatable when the alcoholic first enters treatment, it is often obvious months later. A good deal of this is because family members are rarely confronted with their addictions, and when they are they are allowed to believe it is the addict's fault that they are in pain. Until this changes, people like Sarah will continue to live in their addictive pain with little chance to face their own patterns.

As a rule of thumb, we can assume that adult family members of an alcohol, sex, work, or any other addicted family will have the same number of addictions as the one identified as needing treatment. They will also have a parallel history of focusing on those addictions that seemed to work best in their lives within the context of all their relationships.

In a marriage, whenever one of them drops a shared addiction there will be a history of tension until the other one drops an addiction too. This mutual focusing will occur until they find it impossible to maintain a balance of at least three addictions each for a total of six, or until one of them starts to recover.

The children will also be in the process of developing addictive complexes of their own, having learned addictive coping from the society at large, and from both their parents. When you consider contact time, the child of addictive parents learns more addictive beliefs from the person usually labeled the co-dependent, than from the person labeled the "primary addict." The child often can't recognize this fact because the co-dependent is usually involved with the children in addictive relationships and is the one the child views as his only source of emotional support.

In many families, both of the parents are "fighting through the child" and the co-dependent may be unconsciously setting the child up for problems with the primary addict. This often sets the stage for physical abuse of one child by the alcoholic, while the other children escape such abuse.

Another complication with this issue, is our society's value preferences regarding addictions. As I stated in the addictions chapters, relationship, food, and work addictions are "good" but alcoholism is not. Neither is sex and gambling addiction, nor, to a lesser degree, spending addiction.

Some churches and cults require you to approach your religion in the same manner that an alcoholic drinks in order to be a good church member. In this setting, and many others, we deny with the addicts, their addictions to socially acceptable addictive behaviors, no matter how harmful these addictions are to the person and to his family.

In studying addictions, we should minimize moral judgments. We need to limit our inquiry to the following areas.

*1. Which addictions do these people have?*
*2. What are the patterns within and between the people?*
*3. How much pain is being caused?*
*4. How can they best learn to live in a more loving,*
   *less addictive, manner?*

To side with the food addict against the alcoholic will not ease recovery for either one of them, especially the food addict. Our responsibility is to identify each addiction in a non-judgmental manner, and point them out to all involved. In this way, all are confronted equally in an attempt to upset their power-related judging behavior. Then everyone has a better chance of recovery.

**The Children's Patterns**

Children who are stuck in addictive systems are unable to see healthy manners of coping with stressors. They see the patterns of their parents and other adults in their lives and become somewhat limited in their perceptions of coping options.

For years, in the alcoholism literature, in discussions of family "roles" in alcoholic families, others have described this problem. No matter what the addictions in the family, the children of addicted persons tend to share the addictive coping options modeled by their parents, with the oldest child getting the "good" addictions, and the second oldest getting the "bad" addictions.

Sarah and Doug had two children, both adolescents. The son, Mike, was working at a restaurant, seeing a girl (a daughter of two alcoholic parents), and struggling with his weight. He was seventeen. His fourteen-year-old sister, Ann, was already drinking with her friends, being promiscuous with the boys at her school, and involved in a steady relationship with a boy from another school who was very jealous and possessive. They were creating their parents worlds, only reversing the sex roles.

Mike, the older, is already symbolizing that which is "good" about the family and becoming, in Sharon Wegscheider's terms, the "family hero." Unfortunately, he developed the food addiction too. It was the least destructive of the parents' two substance addictions. Ann is symbolizing everything bad about the family and is becoming Wegscheider's "family scapegoat." She is expanding the relationship addictive patterns to include addictive sexuality, an early pattern in her father's life. Both children chose roles which served to distract the parents from their responsibility in the development of family problems, and allowed the parents to blame all family problems on the scapegoat, Ann, while using the success of the hero, Mike, to convince themselves they are good parents.

Depending on personality factors, children may trade these roles. The oldest two children will almost always develop these roles initially. If there had been other children, they would have either looked outside for models and become "lost" or stayed underdeveloped "mascots" until one of the older two children left. Then they would have competed for one of the two primary roles.

In a family with parents like Doug and Sarah, the hero will usually adopt three family-based addictive coping options: *work, relationships, and food*. The scapegoat will usually adopt the other three: *alcohol, relationships, and sex*. They may not develop these addictions, but they will always have them as dominant options in their coping menus.

In a way these two are the lucky ones. Younger children in the family have difficulty developing any consistent coping style at all, as the five coping options modeled by the parents are taken by their older siblings. The third youngest will often seek out other families and become "lost" to the family's value system, while the fourth becomes the "mascot," a kind of human family pet.

This is perhaps the most painful pattern in addiction. The multi-generational nature of addiction is shown in every addictive family. The experience of living in an addictive home handicaps us in our awareness of coping options available within our society.

In order to choose positive alternatives one must be aware of positive alternatives. Many of my clients who were raised in addictive homes never developed non-addictive alternatives in their perception of reality. This left them handicapped. This is being recognized now with a focus on adult children of alcoholics and co-dependency, but support is only beginning to develop for those whose parents may have had less dramatic or obvious addictions.

In my experience, the problems with maturation for a person with a sex-addictive or even work-addictive family may be either more severe or less severe than the problems for a person from an alcoholic family.

For example, I had a case in which a teenage daughter was so embarrassed and upset over finding out that her father had sex with one of her best friends that she committed suicide at age fourteen. She had known that her father was seeing other adult women and had even helped keep it a secret. Her guilt for being a part of the deception was overwhelming when it affected her friend. All this occurred in spite of the father never having had sex with his daughter.

The severity of the addiction, not the specific addiction, is the deciding factor in the severity of the children's handicaps. They grow into the co-dependency pattern and usually practice addictive relationships with their parents from an early age, no matter what the other addictions in the family may be.

Looking at co-dependents as addicts whose addictions complement those of the other family members, allows family members to understand why they need their own recovery programs. And it interferes with their blaming each other for causing pain which really stems from each individual's own addictions. This understanding is particularly useful when children are involved, because both parents can purposefully develop better coping options while they are recovering from their own addictions, thus broadening their children's own awareness of coping options.

This model also makes it possible for us to recover more effectively from our addictions, whether family members are available or not. It does so precisely because it is a comprehensive model of addiction, helping free us from reactionary patterns by addressing our relationship addictions. In doing so, we can recover from the family illness and gain more independence from the patterns of our childhood.

I hope that considering all the members of an addictive family as having addictions will be useful for you. If you have identified your addictions, but are feeling confused by your family's reactions, it is probably because you are confronting their denial about their own addictions. You do not need to change your family members. That is part of your relationship addiction. You only need to recover from your own addictions and learn to deal with your family in a manner which allows you to see what they face and love them anyway.

If you are in a recovery program, encourage your family to be a part of it, but avoid becoming attached to whether or not they agree to do so. Families are delicate groups, and it takes much skill and care to work with them successfully. We can't fix our own families. If they won't work with you, you will have to work without them.

Also, avoid getting trapped in family guilt patterns which will arise because you are changing. Family members, in defending their own addictive relationship with you, will try to remind you of the past in order to maintain a morally powerful position. When this starts, the best option is to leave, and preferably find a meeting, or a self-help sponsor. Be kind to your family members. Remember, they have addictions of their own.

In any case, this awareness of the addictions of others in your family can help you know how you reached the point in which you needed help in the first place. It can also help you understand the changes in relationships which occur in the early part of your recovery. This can greatly reduce your anxiety.

One of the most artful aspects of addictions is the manner in which addicted persons find and develop addictive relationships with each other. Daughters of alcoholics can marry someone who barely drinks and watch him develop into an alcoholic within the next few years. Relationship and sex addicts recognize each other instantly, are attracted to each other, and automatically know how to connect with each other. We are just beginning to see how this works. When you look at all the players in the drama as equal players, instead of as victims, persecutors, and rescuers, you can see the patterns more clearly.

No matter what our addictions, or our roles in the drama, we are responsible for creating the pain in our lives which results from addictive coping. If you are living or working with someone who is an addict, and to whom you react by feeling crazy, look at your part in the drama, and at your own addictions. This is the only way to begin moving towards sanity.

## For Your Personal Growth

*Looking back at your childhood, did either of your parents drink too much, work too much, eat too much, or have some other addictive pattern? Now remember the patterns of the parent which you did not first identify as having a pattern. What did this parent do in response to the spouse's addictive behavior? Was this behavior addictive or irresponsible? Now explore your own relationships. Do you use someone's behavior in your life to justify irresponsible or unloving behavior of your own? Do others in your life react to your behavior with overeating, drinking, etc.? How do your patterns of behavior fit with theirs?*

# THE TERRITORY

*Our experience has been that, when people come to us in therapy, they typically come with pain, feeling themselves paralyzed, experiencing no choices or freedom of action in their lives. What we have found is not that the world is too limited or that there are no choices, but that these people block themselves from seeing those options and possibilities that are open to them since they are not available in their models of their world.*

                                  - Richard Bandler and John Grinder

Now that I have described addiction and the addictive process, the next natural subject would seem to be recovery from this process. This is our next topic of concern, but, before we move on to recovery, we need to explore where addiction fits into the larger scheme of human consciousness and behavior. So far, we have proceeded from specific addictions to the whole of addictive process. Next, we jump from addictive process to larger concerns of human growth and evolution and where this addictive process fits.

    Throughout this discussion, I have held that addiction is an outcome of flawed maps of reality. We misunderstand the emotional "territory" which we try to explore in our lives and find ourselves in the pattern of addictive coping, pursuing one "dead end" after another. I have also made the case that people develop these flawed maps by adopting values and behavior which are "normal" within Western society. We are all at risk from the very culture we live in.

One core belief held by many therapists, including myself, is that people are almost always doing the best they know how within their model of reality. In everyone's life, there is an internal rationality to behavior regardless of how insane the behavior appears to an observer, or even to the person doing the behaving. Addictive behavior is no exception to this rule. The addictive behavior has some basis in the addicted person's model of reality because it has a basis in our cultural model of reality. In order for someone's behavior to change and remain changed, a shift needs to occur within the model. We have the responsibility for our own welfare, regardless of the threat from the outside world.

All coping behavior is an attempt to cross the territory of our lives. As the result of their addictions, addicts often believe that their needs and lives are somehow different from other's. While their lives are different, it is usually because they behave in manners which retard their normal growth and development and allow others to outperform them at the basic task of maturing or "growing up." Their basic emotional needs are those of the rest of the world.

## States of Consciousness

If this is so, then how can they ever catch up with others in their environment? In the years of observing my own recovery process and the recovery processes of several others, it has become obvious to me that the change that occurs in successful recovery is one in the person's consciousness, his basic philosophies of life and meaning. The nature of that change is from a fear-based "survival" consciousness to a love-based "being" consciousness. This change occurs over a period of years and is necessary in order for the addict to become stable in recovery.

For several years, I couldn't understand how addiction fit in human consciousness, but eventually it came together thanks to my wife. About the time I began writing this book, she brought me a gift. The gift was a book by Gerald Jampolsky, M.D., titled *Love Is Letting Go Of Fear*. In this book, and in his others, Dr.

Jampolsky states that there are only two feeling states, love and fear. In first reading this idea, it seemed patently ridiculous to state that we only had two feelings. He also stated that love was our natural state, and that we were operating in illusion when we operated out of fear. This idea also seemed simplistic. Yet, despite these objections, the concepts in his book were consistent with my observations of reality and I felt a need to resolve the paradox this presented.

I resolved the paradox by taking the "either-or" concept of love or fear which Jampolsky proposed and expanding it into a continuum, which seemed to me to work very well. The idea followed of using love and fear as "categories" or "types" of feelings which other feelings would fall under. The resulting continuum is shown below.

< --------FEAR----------------------------------------LOVE-------- >

*Abject Terror*                                    *Absolute Joy*

All feelings of fear and isolation would exist on the left end of the continuum, and all feelings of love and connectedness would exist on the right end. Anxiety, anger, frustration, and depression would be located at points on the fear side of the continuum. Joy, happiness, calmness, and serenity would be on the love side of the continuum. Neutral feelings would exist in the middle.

One can label the consciousness of the person on the left end of the continuum of feelings as "survival consciousness" and the consciousness of the person on the right end of the continuum as "being consciousness."

Survival consciousness is that stage of consciousness in which one views the world as a hostile place, and sees his role as being on constant guard to ensure his own survival. Central to this world view is a constant belief that one is a victim or potential victim. The person at this level of consciousness is just trying to survive. Actions taken at this level have the goal of satisfying needs or wants.

Being consciousness is that stage of consciousness in which one views the world as a loving place, and acts lovingly and creatively towards self and others. Central to this world view is a belief in being creative. The person at this level of consciousness is preoccupied with being happy and loving. Actions at this level focus on selfless giving.

After developing these descriptions, I modified the description as follows:

< --------FEAR-----------------------------------------LOVE-------- >

*Abject Terror * Survival Consciousness * Being Consciousness * Nirvana*

Among the conclusions that can be drawn from this model of feelings is that *we often function at survival consciousness even though no threat to our survival exists*. We act in ways which may seem rational in view of a real threat, but which are irrational if no threat, in truth, exists. Whether we feel fear or love determines where we are on the continuum and the level of consciousness we experience. The greater the *perceived threat*, the more defensive the behavior of the person who is perceiving. When we are practicing an addiction we are operating in this state of survival consciousness.

We all make mistakes in our perception of threat, and this has sometimes resulted in our acting with inappropriate defensiveness. For example, the police in my locale just arrested a man who had robbed ten banks over a period of several months and had successfully carted away thousands of dollars even though he had only carried a plastic pistol. At first, this seemed surprising until I put myself in the position of the bank employee who was being robbed. It became much easier to understand how someone could convince me not to question whether the perceived danger was real, and how I would give the robber anything he wanted. My fear would be real, even though the threat was bogus. My perception of reality, not true reality, would dictate my behavior. My giving him the money would appear "rational" both to me and any observer who agreed with my perception of threat. The robber knew this, and took advantage of his knowledge, ten times with ten people.

**Fear and Addiction**

An addictive behavior pattern is similar to the bank employee's. It usually starts with fear resulting from an inaccurate definition of a current or potential problem. The person involved in the behavior imagines that the "problem" is causing uncomfortable feelings, and sets out to solve the problem by changing the feelings.

**Taming The "Green Monster."** *John, a client of mine, was very jealous. Whenever he was unable to directly observe his wife's behavior he began to feel jealous and imagine that she was having an affair. He would get very upset and drink to deal with his feelings. Then, when he would see his wife, he would be drunk and irrational and blame her for his irrational feelings and behavior. Instead of facing his fear and dealing with his problem of jealousy, he used addictive behavior to treat his feelings and deny his problem.*

*The first part of therapy consisted of convincing him that his wife did not want to leave him or have an affair, but that his irrational behavior would make it difficult for anyone to deal with him and might lead to divorce. He also came to realize that his real problem was his deep-seated feelings of being unlovable. Then, he was able to begin the process of change. Once he could believe that his wife wanted to stay with him he could see how crazy he had been acting.*

Addictive behavior seems perfectly rational to the person involved, but it is an irrational problem-solving method. Competent problem-solving requires first that a problem be well-defined and second that the problem, not the side-effects of the problem, be the focus of attack.

Survival consciousness, in any part of our life, makes it difficult to distinguish between real and imagined threat, and produces constant free-floating anxiety. The anxiety produces an internal focus on feelings and further vagueness of thought. This confusion, in turn, is often treated with fix-oriented behaviors. Since the fix-oriented behavior does nothing to confront the survival consciousness, and constitutes a giving in to fearful perception, the fear is validated by the attempt to treat it.

## Core Beliefs Revisited

Earlier in the book, I stated that addicts had a core belief that happiness exists at a physical level and is achievable by their own direct action. This false belief is the core belief of someone in survival consciousness. This is a power-based way of viewing the world and produces feelings of isolation which, in turn, produce fear.

I also stated that people in recovery come to believe they can achieve happiness as a side-effect of dedicating themselves to something greater than ourselves and to loving interaction with other people. This is the core belief which evolves as we move from survival consciousness to being consciousness.

So fear-based survival consciousness starts with addictive core beliefs and love-based being consciousness starts with the recovery core beliefs. Let's review the diagram with this added:

```
<--------FEAR----------------------------------------LOVE-------->
```

*Survival Consciousness*        *Being Consciousness*
*Terror*                        *Nirvana (Absolute Joy)*
*Addictive Core Belief*         *Recovery Core Belief*

We can see a pattern evolving in which recovery and maturity both reflect a movement from the fear-based to the love-based end of the continuum.

## Developmental Psychology

The discovery of Jampolsky's ideas and the following development of the feeling continuum and the concepts of survival consciousness helped me to gain some perspective, and reminded me of my studies in developmental psychology. Developmental psychology is a branch of psychology which explores the normal emotional and mental development of people as they age and mature. It is, in other words, a field of psychology which studies the territory of our mental/emotional development so that we can have an accurate understanding of how humans mature. This field has existed for several years and has produced quite accurate models or maps of this territory.

This is relevant because addicts have no different patterns of development than others. They merely spend much of their time walking in circles when they need to be maturing.

The following ideas are a synthesis of models of development offered by Maslow, Kohlberg, Erikson, Sheehy, Keyes, and Hall. Developmental psychology is a well-developed science, and we will simply explore where addictive behavior fits in this scheme of human development and consciousness.

Let us review the model of feelings and consciousness presented earlier:

< --------FEAR----------------------------------------LOVE-------- >

| | |
|---|---|
| *Survival Consciousness* | *Being Consciousness* |
| *Terror* | *Nirvana (Absolute Joy)* |
| *Addictive Core Belief* | *Recovery Core Belief* |

In this model, we can experience feelings from abject terror to absolute joy. In consciousness terms, that means we can concern ourselves with survival or simply being, but we can't focus on both together. We can, however, shift from one end of this continuum to another instantly. Obviously, feeling fear prohibits feeling love at the same instant. I believe the process of maturation results in spending more and more time on the love end of the continuum and less and less time on the fear end. As we grow, we follow an emotional path from the left to the right end of this continuum. So we can add maturation to the diagram:

< --------FEAR----------------------------------------LOVE-------- >

| | |
|---|---|
| *Survival Consciousness* | *Being Consciousness* |
| *Terror* | *Nirvana (Absolute Joy)* |
| *Addictive Core Belief* | *Recovery Core Belief* |

--------------------------MATURATION------------------------- >

Central to this model is the belief that we define who we are in reaction to our perception of the threatening or loving nature of the external world. Those in survival consciousness view the world in hostile terms. Those in being consciousness view the world in loving terms. This is consistent with the concept that we deal with our model of reality, rather than with reality directly.

Whatever we do in life is done within the context of the larger schemes of development and maturity. Developmental theory, as a whole, shows that a view of the world as a hostile place reflects the lower stages of human development. The more loving the person's world view, the farther he or she has progressed in individual development. We can all be found within this range of growth. For this reason, we can use a model of human development to describe the internal territory within which we pursue the quests of our lives.

Most developmental theorists break down their stages of consciousness into six to eight separate periods. At one time, theorists proposed that these stages were fairly rigid and final. Now, most theorists agree that we move back and forth between levels of maturity and spend higher percentages of our time in higher levels of development with forays back into less mature states under stress. It appears that maturing consists of spending less and less time in fear-based functioning, but returning to such functioning under overwhelming stress until we can achieve relative serenity in spite of stressors.

Some authors describe their developmental concepts in terms of stages of consciousness, as opposed to stages of development. This seems to work very well. We all have the ability to start a day feeling loving and competent and end the day feeling like a frustrated child. The secret of maturing is to stay as emotionally stable as possible. So maturing coincides with spending more time on the loving end of the feeling continuum and less time on the fear end. We can go back and forth in our consciousness each day, but once we develop a model of reality which works consistently, we will be less afraid.

One of the basic tenets of human development theories, regardless of the theorist, is that we have a natural drive or need to mature and that the path of our maturity will be from one of dependence on others to independence to interdependence with others and the world. Addiction represents dependence on others, behaviors, or substances. This must eventually be outgrown if we are to mature happily. Addiction, therefore is automatically integrated into our maturation process.

Given what we know about human development, I can propose a model of how our concerns change as we move from fearful to loving feelings throughout our day, and throughout our lives. In combining the models of the others I have mentioned and my own experience, I propose an eight-level consciousness/development model. The first three stages of consciousness will be familiar to you. The stages are:

1. *Security/Survival.* During our early years, we are in very vulnerable states. We are concerned with our ability to exist without others feeding and clothing us. The earliest developmental task is to learn to trust that our needs will be met. If we fail to learn this, we can be concerned with security and survival the rest of our lives. So, even as adults, we can be constantly trying to assure that we will not be abandoned. If we never leave this state of mind, we will never be able to progress in our consciousness. Being stuck in this constant security/survival level of consciousness is the most fearful and can be terrorizing.

2. *Sensation.* Once we feel we are relatively safe, we progress to concerns of sensation and pleasure. We begin to explore how we can have various feelings, including those of power and control over others to the extent that we can ensure pleasure. We are still fearful when we don't get our way, and we still do not love, but we do begin to move in that direction.

3. *Power/Order.* At this stage of our thinking, we are concerned with control over self and others. We tend to be very focused on "rules," especially as a means of keeping others in line with our beliefs. We believe that everything should be in a certain order, and see ourselves as guardians of that order. We experience fear when our order doesn't occur, and when we are unable to live up to our own standards.

**4.** *Peer Identification.* In this stage we define ourselves by the nature of our relationships with others, and focus on achievement and the beginnings of self-expression. We are still focused on following rules on a personal level, but experience confusion in leadership positions. This is the major stage of transition from Survival Consciousness to Being Consciousness. People at this level have a difficult time being consistent with their children or being assertive with their friends. They shift back and forth frequently from loving to fearful feelings. The major task in this stage is the development of trust in others outside of those in authority.

**5.** *Individuality.* Self love and confidence are the most consistent goals of the person in this stage of development. Establishing appropriate boundaries between self and others occurs here. We also become concerned with such issues as service to others and equality.

**6.** *Creating.* At this stage, we create our lives in self-actualizing manners. We pursue creative projects, preferably with others. Intimacy becomes a primary concern. Human dignity is very important to us at this stage and we see the world as a project to improve.

**7.** *Visionary.* Primary values at this level are spiritual. The visionary person explores both intimacy and solitude, as well as the interdependence of all life. They tend to be prophets in their fields. They develop many of the maps for the growth of others.

**8.** *Saints.* There aren't many of these. Mother Theresa, Gandhi, Saint Francis, and other persons we recognize as being somehow evolved beyond the rest of us are in this stage. Very few of us will reach it. In spite of this, we can study them and use them as examples of our human potential. Very few of us will stay on the lower end of the continuum, but very few of us will reach the highest levels. Most of us peak at levels three to five in our development, with most of our institutions operating at levels three and four. Even most of our religious institutions focus on the rules of the third and fourth levels of value development. Our cultural evolution has not reached the level where it is no longer survival-oriented. This inhibits the personal development of us all.

Now, let's combine this model with the feelings continuum:

< --------FEAR----------------------------------------LOVE-------- >

*Survival Consciousness*          *Being Consciousness*
*Terror*                          *Nirvana (Absolute Joy)*
*Addictive Core Belief*           *Recovery Core Belief*

--------------------------MATURATION-------------------------- >

*Security -Sensation -Power/Order -Peer Ident -Individlty -Creating -Visionary -Saint*

As you can see, the models complement each other well. The feeling of absolute joy is the feeling state associated with *sainthood*, and terror coordinates with the feelings of the *security* level of functioning. The shift from survival consciousness to being consciousness occurs during the *peer identification* phase of development.

As we grow and mature, we have a natural tendency to move from the fear end to the love end of the continuum. Addictive behavior is even used to explore the lower three stages of consciousness so that we can move on to more mature functioning. If the addictive behavior progresses to an addiction, however, it slows down the natural pace of a person's maturation. As addictive behavior keeps us locked into searches for security, sensation, and power, the time we commit to our addictions prevents us from committing time to more mature, loving functioning. It keeps us in survival consciousness.

**Survival Consciousness**

Most of us occasionally feel that the world is hostile, and view ourselves as victims of certain institutions and persons. Therefore, we operate at least part of the time, in the first three stages of consciousness. Everyone moves back and forth between stages, tending to stabilize at one level most of the time.

Operation within the survival level of consciousness well into adolescence is normal. As small children, we are primarily concerned with security issues. During ages five to around twelve we explore sensation issues. Then, during adolescence, we delve into power/control issues until we launch from our families. At that time, we need to start outgrowing these levels of functioning and complete our sense of individuality.

For the person who habitually copes addictively, this growth process is retarded. This retardation occurs because all addictive behavior focuses on providing feelings appropriate to childhood stages. This denies the experiences needed to progress to higher stages of evolution. Addictive coping pulls backward toward emotional patterns appropriate for a younger person.

The chronically addicted person operates at one of the lower three levels virtually all the time: security, sensation, or power/order. He moves from the lowest level to the third level as he advances in his addiction, but very slowly.

To live in the lower three levels of consciousness is to live with a constant sense of vulnerability. This is fearful and serves as a constant emotional pain. Addictive, fix-oriented behavior seems rational within this level of consciousness, much like pain medication is rational to treat a chronic toothache. But since the pain arises out of our own perceptions of reality, it is very difficult to become convinced that the pain can go away.

Until we outgrow this sense of vulnerability and develop a sense of our own independence, fix-oriented behavior will seem rational to us. Furthermore, when we regress back into these levels of consciousness under stress, the addictive behavior will again look attractive.

We need to look to our own emotional development as the cornerstone of understanding, leaving addictive behavior behind. Although addiction can be a part of our developmental process, it is an extremely slow way to grow and many addicts die before they get past survival consciousness levels of emotional maturity.

As I described earlier, our societal institutions model the lower levels of functioning. It is our individual perception, however, which allows the freedom to live in a survival state or a being state. We are always free to choose! We need to learn the healthy lessons our culture offers, while recognizing those lessons which offer nothing but misery.

*For Your Personal Growth*

*Review the stages of consciousness and assess where you are most of the time. We will move back and forth, but most of the time we will be in one of these stages of consciousness. Apply this description of consciousness stages to your family. Assess which view of the world the individuals are taught within this system. Apply the same description to your workplace or school. How are you expected to view yourself in relationship to the world in each of these settings?*

*Review the continuum of feelings in this chapter, and ask yourself which end of the continuum reflects your normal emotional state. Do you find yourself interpreting most situations in your life as threatening? Do you like the pattern you discern? Review the two core belief systems outlined in the chapter and ask which belief is close to your own beliefs. They are presented as extremes, so you may not believe either of them exactly, but the closer you are to the recovery beliefs, the more contented you are likely to be in your life.*

# RECOVERY:

# THE  NEW  FRONTIER

*If I had only...*
*forgotten future greatness*
*and looked at the green things and the buildings*
*and reached out to those around me*
*and smelled the air*
*and ignored the forms and self-styled obligations*
*and heard the rain on the roof*
*and put my arms around my wife*
*. . . and it's not too late.*
- Hugh Prather

As I described in the last chapter, the pattern of change in recovery is one of moving from fear-based *Survival Consciousness* to love-based *Being Consciousness*. This is not a major change in direction in a person's development, but rather, the continuing of a developmental process which was slowed or halted by addiction.

To prepare for the recovery path ahead of those who *do* successfully give up addictive coping, let's review the developmental model presented in the previous chapter. The complete model looked like this:

```
< -------FEAR-------------------------------------LOVE-------- >
```

*Survival Consciousness*          *Being Consciousness*
*Terror*                          *Nirvana (Absolute Joy)*
*Addictive Core Belief*           *Recovery Core Belief*

```
-------------------------MATURATION------------------------- >
```

*Security -Sensation -Power/Order -Peer Ident -Individlty -Creating -Visionary -Saint*

The previous sections of the book have described how Survival Consciousness related to addiction. The next section will concern itself with moving into Being Consciousness. So the focus is on the Peer Identity stages through the higher stages of functioning. I have described the territory of addiction, now I will describe the territory of recovery.

**Being Consciousness**

We have discussed Survival Consciousness, now let's explore Being Consciousness more completely.  For anyone trying to understand recovery from addiction, this type of consciousness is the territory ahead.

Looking at the love end of the continuum, we have:

**Love**

```
-----------Being Consciousness---------- >
```
*Neutral*                                      *Absolute Joy*

**Recovery Core Beliefs**

```
--------------------------Maturity----------------------- >
```
Peer Ident.  Individuality  Creating  Visionary  Saint

Recovery consists of maturing first from Survival to Being Consciousness, then proceeding to more advanced levels within this consciousness. This is the appropriate developmental movement for us anyway. We give up our addictions because they prevent this healthy maturation from occurring.

There are no short cuts to maturing. Each stage of development serves as the foundation of the following stages. We need to accept, throughout our lives, that we can only move so quickly. We can speed up our maturation by adopting, on faith, the recovery core beliefs, but growth and change take time.

It is obvious from this model that, before we can concern ourselves with higher levels of development, we each have to complete the communal tasks and develop an independent identity. We need to make the jump from mistrusting, unloving, and isolated ways of living to learning to be communal creatures. This requires involvement with others in attempts to grow. Any attempts to "do it myself" only reflect a continuing belief in self-control and power. This is the first belief which must be outgrown in recovery.

For several years now, the source of peer experience and help in the beginning shift from Survival to Being Consciousness for most addicts has been self-help groups. Most of these groups, such as Alcoholics Anonymous, are based on a "twelve-step program" which is a systematic method of developing and reinforcing the recovery core beliefs mentioned here. These groups were founded by persons attempting to recover and represent the most significant developments to date for persons dealing with addictions.

Once we involve ourselves with others, we must work to develop a sense of individual identity. We do this in concert with others who provide necessary feedback regarding our new beliefs and identity. Treatment programs and self-help groups offer the opportunities needed to refine our beliefs about ourselves.

Once someone develops an individual sense of identity, he is hooked. While addiction is useful only for relieving the pain of Survival Consciousness, growth stages within higher levels of consciousness are self-reinforcing. Everyone wants to go further. Love is its own reward.

Because of this, once one is grounded in the Individuality stage of development, he will want to continue the involvement with others in developing the sense of interdependence which signifies the Creating stage. In this involvement, for the first time in the addict's life, he learns to love in healthy ways. He becomes the sponsor or senior group member, for example, paving the way for others and helping them in their quests. He may go on to develop the high levels of spirituality of the Visionary stage.

So, in order to recover from addictions, we need to quit using addictive coping, which doesn't work anyway, and proceed on a path of growth and maturation which is our natural path and which offers us a chance at true serenity. What could be more natural than that?

## Resistance

In spite of the natural, positive path ahead in recovery, most people have trouble making the changes necessary to switch from addictive coping to more productive coping styles. It is quite difficult to accept that core beliefs in one's map of reality are inaccurate. We can become confused and anxious even considering such a possibility.

So it only follows that when most of my clients come to see me, they are there to deal, in one way or another, with one addiction. They sincerely believe that their lives will be just fine if they can either quit the addiction, or, more usually, get it under control.

These people know that drinking, sex, food, relationships, or some other painful addiction is causing them problems. They want to change that fact, while going on with business as usual in the rest of their lives. They believe they can solve the problem of a faulty map of reality, by simply deciding not to use one road anymore. This doesn't work, but it is an excellent place to start.

No one simply stops being addictive. Recovering from addictions is complicated because quitting all our addictions when we believe in addictive coping is to stop having a coping strategy in our model of reality. In order to be successful, the recovering addict will have to develop new strategies and practice them until they seem "real."

**The Road Ahead**

Say, just for the sake of argument, that you have identified addiction(s) in your life. You want to recover from those addictions and you want to know how. For most people, there are three stages to recovery: Treatment, early or *Stage I Recovery*, and advanced or *Stage II Recovery*. Treatment is necessary in advanced addiction or disease-level progression. It lasts anywhere from a month to two years. Almost all advanced addicts can benefit from ongoing treatment for a one-year minimum. In addictive disease, medical care is necessary. Medical consultation should occur if there are physical withdrawals from an addiction. Overlapping treatment, when it is required, continues for at least one year (usually two to five years) in early or Stage I Recovery. In this process, we are simply focused on learning how to deal with our addictions, developing stable abstinence, and building some minimal new social supports. We also begin development of more loving social and spiritual perspectives.

During this period of time, recovery needs to be the highest priority in the recovering person's life. This stage occurs most effectively through participation in peer support groups, the most effective of which are based on the twelve steps originally used by Alcoholics Anonymous.

After we are stable in our early recovery, we automatically move into the issues of Stage II Recovery. These issues are psychological development and building a lifestyle which provides health and serenity. It is at this stage that we genuinely begin to enjoy life, perhaps for the first time. Unfortunately, many addicts quit working on themselves before they get this far. If they do so, they fall short of achieving the only rational goal of this whole recovery process.

**Serenity**

No matter what the addiction, the primary goal of recovery is the achievement of serenity, peace of mind. Quitting our addictions is not the primary goal. Rather, it is only a sub-objective of the goal of serenity.

When we quit addictive coping we do so only because the outcome of such coping is misery, insanity, or death. We want to be happy, not miserable. Why else go through the pain of dealing with the addiction(s) at all? So peace of mind is the primary goal of the successfully recovering person and, in my opinion, of any of us who are thinking clearly.

Peace of mind is also the goal of addictive behavior. A serene internal emotional state is something everyone wants. In addiction, we are merely going in the wrong direction in the serenity search.

Earlier in the book, I said that using addiction as a meaning search was like trying to drive from Indianapolis to San Diego by heading northeast towards Boston. The person in this situation may strongly desire to reach San Diego, but he is travelling by the wrong route. Likewise, the addicted person wants serenity, but is going the wrong way rapidly. The severely addicted person doesn't even take in the sights along the way. If the traveler is ever going to get to San Diego, first he has to turn around. After he turns around, he has some distance to make up just to get back to his starting point. So it is with recovering from addictions. Before the addict can recover, he must first turn around and begin heading in the right direction.

The discovery of appropriate goals and directions can sometimes be the most important thing in life. Many of us are able to proceed directly toward meaningful lives. We learned, from somewhere, to understand what worked in this meaning quest.

Others have to learn the hard way by developing addictions, and "hitting bottom" first. Once we have addictions in our lives, there is no way to avoid experiencing a significant amount of emotional pain. We always hit bottom in some way before we turn our lives around.

**"Hitting Bottom"**

Andy is a recovering alcoholic. He has been sober for several years, but he still remembers the night he decided to stop drinking. He came home from work drunk and started arguing with his wife, which was his usual nightly routine. After the argument, he grabbed a beer, sat in his chair, and invited his eight-year-old daughter to sit on his lap. She refused. He persisted and she looked him in the eyes and stated, "I don't want to. You're mean. You drink too much. You stink. And I don't even like you anymore!" This, for Andy, produced the experience of "hitting bottom."

For Cheryl, it was the morning she ripped her favorite dress trying to put it on. She had gained so much weight that it wouldn't go on. Denying this, she tried to force herself into it and ripped it beyond repair. This was the last straw.

For Ann, it was the look in her son's eyes when her abusive husband threatened to kill him over an issue which was actually between her and her husband. She finally realized how her children had been pawns in their sick relationship. She also realized she had nowhere to go but up.

Throughout the history of addictions treatment, there has been the concept of "hitting bottom." The belief has been that an addict had to experience great pain before deciding to recover from his addictions. Another way of saying this is that our addictive coping patterns must "break our own hearts" before we will fall out of love with them. Andy's daughter helped him to realize that his alcoholism was causing him more pain than pleasure and he entered treatment the next morning. Cheryl and Ann had similar realizations. There are many ways to experience hitting bottom and it is different for each individual.

In addictions treatment, there are ways of "raising someone's bottom" through various confrontational techniques. The fact remains that the pain of addiction usually has to outweigh the pleasure we rerceive before we will start to recover from it.

Hitting bottom, in a larger sense, is coming to the realization that one is going the wrong way in the search for serenity and one is going to have to give up some precious concepts about reality to achieve the goal. This is usually accompanied by severe emotional pain. We believe in, even "love," our addictive options.

When a person experiences this, it reflects that he is finally learning that there is no happiness to be obtained from behaving as though security, sensation, and power are rich sources of meaning. He will only have learned this lesson in reference to his primary addiction(s), but he is on his way. Now he is ready to learn new lessons. Those lessons can only come from continued maturation into more advanced stages of consciousness.

Unless this occurs, the addictive core beliefs will trigger either a return to the current addictive pattern, or a shift to a new, equally fruitless, addictive pattern. This is easy to see for those of you who are familiar with the twelve steps of various self-help programs. The twelve steps teach the core beliefs of recovery and lead us to develop loving relationships. Only the first of the twelve steps deals with the specific addiction a person has. The other eleven train the person to become a more mature, spiritual, loving person.

## Letting Go of the Romance

A part of hitting bottom is facing the prospect of immediate emotional pain. The initial reaction to giving up, or deciding to give up, even one addiction is panic. This panic is normal and it is important that it be understood.

Addicts have feelings towards their addictions. These feelings are feelings of attachment and intensity. The addict experiences these feelings as the closest thing to love in his life. The further an addiction progresses, the more emotional attachment develops to it. Unfortunately, by the time the addiction reaches the disease stage, the relationship intensity is often like that of a pathologically intense relationship with another person. In fact, I can use the intensity of relationship addiction to illustrate this principle of letting go of the romance.

One's relationship with his addiction is always intense. This intensity is the closest feeling to true intimacy that many of us have felt. We often confuse this addictive intensity with intimacy in our romantic relationships. For that reason, first infatuations are very intense. Likewise, the pain of rejection or ending our first romance usually stays in our memories forever.

The addictive romantic relationship has patterns which hold true for any other addiction. When we meet someone with whom we immediately "fall in love," we develop intense feelings rapidly. We proceed from those feelings to build fantasy images of the love object, the other person. We develop rituals which reinforce our belief that the person is indeed all that we fantasized until such a time as reality reveals that he or she is just human. This is often followed by extremely intense withdrawal pain as we give up the relationship.

This pain is not especially reflective of giving up the other person. Rather, it reflects the pain experienced when giving up our fantasies. The reality of the great relationship wasn't there. We mistook intensity for intimacy and confused ourselves. Every addiction operates the same way and causes the same kind of pain.

The pattern of falling in love, intense feelings, fantasy, and painful withdrawal, occurs in any addictive process. There are also rituals which seem to keep the romance alive. The ending of any addiction produces the broken-hearted experience of withdrawal.

This "withdrawal" pain is in store for anyone beginning recovery from addiction(s). Furthermore, he must endure this pain before he can get on with his life. He must let go of the romance in his addictive fantasies and accept the addiction's empty reality. This is a frightening prospect, but he must do it. Recovering people do it all the time because they see no alternative to quitting their addictions if they are to achieve the primary goal of recovery.

### Getting Well

Once we decide to deal with an addiction, we are faced with the choice whether to start another one or to recover from addictive coping and get well. Getting well is the rational choice, but most of us make the other choice several times before we become rational. Once we do decide to get well or recover we follow the recovery process outlined earlier, Treatment, Stage I Recovery, and finally Stage II Recovery. The recovery process is a healing which begins with any needed physical healing, proceeds to mental/ emotional healing, and then to interpersonal/spiritual healing. This recovery "path" is taught in almost every treatment program for addictions in the world.

## Treatment

For those who have progressed to the severe or disease stage of their addictions, treatment is often required at the beginning of recovery. There are currently addictions treatment programs available for alcohol and various drugs, including specialized cocaine units, sex, gambling, eating disorders, and even outpatient addictive relationship programs. There are also mental health programs which regularly deal with side effects of work-addiction and other compulsive disorders. This treatment usually has three stages which occur after the problem is recognized: physical healing, mental/emotional retraining, and interpersonal/spiritual exploration. You can see that this process is consistent with the process of recovery mentioned earlier.

### Physical Healing

Physical healing will automatically begin once we quit abusing our bodies with addictive behavior. Unless we have abused ourselves beyond the body's rejuvenating ability, a certain amount of physical healing will occur. We can and should try to potentiate this process.

The beginning of the physical healing process may be quite painful because physical withdrawal will often be the first experience to overcome. The further the disease has progressed, the longer this process takes. For most addictions with physical withdrawals, treatment is necessary to guarantee safety for some people. This is especially true of chemical addictions. Do not attempt withdrawal from chemical addictions without first consulting a physician.

After withdrawals, the slower process of healing the body from the stress of the addiction begins. If we have progressed to the addiction level with any behavior, the stress of that addiction alone will require this healing. It is exhausting to go through the breakup of an addictive relationship. The exhausted work addict will need a period of rest and recuperation, as well as of reevaluation. The sex addict may have to heal from damage to his sex organs due to abuse and disease, as well as from damage to his body from the stress he has felt for a long time. This healing is almost always necessary.

The components of this healing are the development of good health habits. Diet, exercise, and proper rest are extremely important in this healing process. Diet should be rational and it is a good idea to consult with a physician regarding a need for vitamin supplements. Exercise should be moderate, but regularly scheduled. Addiction is built around rituals. Recovery needs to have replacement rituals of its own. Adequate rest is crucial. With the other demands of recovery, such as self-help attendance and other treatments, it is often difficult to stick to a schedule which provides plenty of rest. Nevertheless, it is necessary.

## Mental/Emotional Retraining

Once the physical healing has stabilized to the point that one can participate in other forms of treatment, treatment centers begin a process of mental/emotional retraining which enables the addict to discover new interpretations of reality and new options for coping with life. This training program is usually based upon the twelve steps, to provide a foundation for continued recovery in twelve step groups. These groups will continue this retraining after release from treatment. The self-centered world view of the addict is explored in depth in almost every treatment program.

Whether it happens during inpatient treatment, outpatient treatment, or only in self-help groups, this level of retraining is critical. Without this retraining, the addict will misunderstand his goals, and focus on quitting the addictions as the only answer. Such magical thinking will lead to continued misery and eventual return to one or more addictions unless he learns new mental/emotional patterns.

## Interpersonal/Spiritual Exploration

During the latter part of treatment, most programs begin to deal with the way the addict relates to the universe. This starts with concepts about relationships and continues into family therapy and discussions about spirituality. This is important. The isolation the addict produces by his interactions with others and with God is responsible for much of the emotional pain of addiction. He has developed a world view based on seeing others and God as being hostile to his existence. This world view must be changed. Trust is essential to mental/emotional and interpersonal/spiritual health. Addicts usually begin exploring this trust issue in treatment.

**Early Recovery**

After treatment, or instead of treatment, these healing themes will need to continue in order to achieve the serenity or peace of mind the addict is working towards. There are some basic things that he needs to do during the early stages of recovery. These tasks are:

*1. Accept that he is powerless over his addiction(s) and that his life becomes unmanageable every time he tries to use addictive coping. He also needs to accept that he will not be able to use addictions in a coping strategy in the future without re-creating the pain he is trying to heal.*

*2. Abstain on a daily basis from any power-level addictions and from any other addictions which are not necessary for survival.*

*3. Consistently work on the growth steps of a twelve-step program as a way of continuing mental/emotional, and spiritual/interpersonal retraining.*

*4. Seek to learn, from sources outside his current network of addictive complements, preferably with other recovering addicts, alternative ways of modeling and coping with reality.*

All these steps are applicable to what some authors call "Stage I Recovery." I will explore these steps, then proceed to more advanced or "Stage II Recovery." I need to begin as the twelve steps do with "Powerlessness."

*For Your Personal Growth*

*Review the core beliefs of addiction and recovery again and reevaluate which one is closest to your beliefs. Review the descriptions of the last five stages of consciousness and see which description best fits your life.*

*Review your conclusions about your addictions and ask if the unhappiness you have received from them is a bad thing to trade for your growth and maturity.*

# POWERLESSNESS

*We came to believe that we were powerless over alcohol, that our lives had become unmanageable.*

- Alcoholics Anonymous

In an early chapter, I made the point that addiction was a reflection of attempts by people to maintain self-control and to achieve happiness at a physical level by direct action. In other words, the addiction signifies a belief on the addict's part in his power over himself and other aspects of the universe. I also made the case that such power was impossible given our status as mortal beings

Since addiction is an outcome of our belief in personal power, it should come as no surprise that the first step of the twelve-step program is concerned with accepting our powerlessness over our addictions. This is the starting part of our retraining in learning to recover from any addiction(s).

## Changing Core Beliefs

This topic of powerlessness goes directly to the changes which are necessary in an addict's core beliefs if he is to recover from addictive coping. The addictive core belief that happiness exists at a physical level and is achievable by direct action on my part logically leads one to take that direct physical action and use illusional power to achieve happiness. If this core belief were true, then happiness or peace of mind would be achievable as the result of imposing our will on the universe around us and addictive behavior would be sane.

On the other hand, the belief that happiness occurs at a love or spirituality level, as a side effect of dedicating ourselves to a "power greater than ourselves" and to others in interdependent relationships, does not lead to the conclusion that we need to impose ourselves on the universe in order to have our needs met. Our task, instead, is to live our lives in a more loving, responsible manner and to trust in others and a *Higher Power* to produce our happiness. The transition from the first set of beliefs to the second set is the underlying process of recovery. The acceptance of powerlessness over our addiction(s) is a very significant step in this transition.

If we explore this further, however, we discover we are not just powerless over our addictions. There is nothing in life over which we have absolute or even consistent power. It is a well-known principle in psychology that trying too hard for control over oneself produces loss of control over one's mental/emotional state. There are several disorders besides addictions which result from obsessive attempts to control ourselves and others.

When one ignores this basic state of powerlessness and proceeds as if he has power over self and others, he produces side effects in himself and in those around him which result in his life becoming more and more unmanageable. The secret is to learn how to flow with life, not how to control life.

### The Tug-of-War

Trying to control ourselves puts us in a psychological position in which parts of us are in a metaphorical tug-of-war with other parts. If you have ever been in a tug-of-war, you know that you had little freedom until you let go of your end of the rope, or until the other person released his end of the rope and you picked yourself up from the ground or the mud. As long as the contest continued, you had little freedom of movement.

Accepting powerlessness over your addiction(s) is like cutting your end of the rope which you use to try to pull your addictive self into line. Once the rope is cut, the addiction loses its power over you. Urges to return to your addiction represent the addictive part of yourself taunting you to pick up the other end of the rope again and start tugging on yourself.

Trying to control others also sets up a tug-of-war with those others in which none of the participants have any true freedom until someone cuts the rope. We see this in relationship addictions or co-dependent relationships when the spouse of an addict goes to a twelve-step program or treatment and learns to "detach" from the other person's addictions. This detachment is nothing more than cutting the imaginary rope which keeps the "co-addict" in a psychological tug-of-war with the "addict." It works very well, allowing one person to recover regardless of the other person's actions.

I stated earlier that all addiction reflects the quests for power in the forms of security, sensation, and direct control over life. Powerlessness recognizes that there is no meaning in power and allows us to look for the freedom that occurs when we progress beyond power-based to love-based functioning. I would like to take this concept, explore it, and expand upon a model of behavior which I presented earlier.

### An Expanded Model

Let us review the model of addictive coping presented in the Introduction. It stated that people had problems which led to symptoms which in turn often lead to a decision to treat the symptoms with addictive behavior.

**Problem----->Symptoms----->Treatment**

While treatment could be aimed at either the actual problem or the symptoms, the point was made that treatment of problems was more appropriate.

Since working with Dr. Glenn, I have become dissatisfied with this model. It is accurate at one level, but inaccurate at another. The truth is that we have a much more complex decision-making process about addictive behavior. The idea of whether we deserve to have power over the universe is crucial to the actual complexity of this issue. Let's review an expanded version of the earlier model.

**Reality-->*Map Of Reality*-->Feeling-->*Map Of Reality*-->Action**

|  |  |
|---|---|
| *Power-Based* | *Power-Based* |
| *vs.* | *vs.* |
| *Love-Based* | *Love-Based* |

In truth, whether we define something in our lives as a problem is usually dependent on our maps of reality. If we have a power-based map of reality, we perceive almost any situation in which we do not get our way as a problem. This definition occurs within our maps of reality. Once we invent a problem, symptoms (usually uncomfortable feelings) result.

On the other hand, if we have a love-based model of reality, we define very few situations as being worthy of emotional duress. If we do not need to control situations so that we get our way, we seldom create uncomfortable feelings, and when we do, we are likely to be more accurate in our perception.

Feelings or symptoms are always the result of power-based judgements which we derive from our map of reality. When our life is threatened, the symptoms of fear and anxiety lead us to appropriate action. This is rational. When we produce the same symptoms simply because life isn't giving us what we want, this is irrational and inappropriate. We produce our feelings by the judgement we make. This may happen so fast that we are unaware of it, but it always happens.

For example, for years I had the belief that working hard and doing a good job would result in a feeling of acceptance. When I would start on a new job, I would set out to do the best job I could and wait for the inevitable strokes to come from my peers and supervisors who would admire my ambition.

Unfortunately, my obsessive drive for acceptance was often taken for extreme competitiveness and this alienated my peers. My supervisors often noticed this and were uncomfortable about the staff friction and occasionally interpreted that I was out for their jobs. My attempts to control my acceptance by others produced rejection.

After I started dealing with my work addiction, I began to work at a more reasonable pace and spend more time nurturing interpersonal relationships with my peers. I also stopped looking for validation from my superiors and simply accepted what came along. As the result of this, I developed better peer relationships and received praise for both my fitting in with the group and my job performance. Once I trusted that I didn't need to guarantee my acceptance by power-based behaviors, acceptance came as a side-effect of more loving interaction on my part. This was a powerful lesson. For years, I had been defining the reactions of others as problems when they didn't respond positively to my attempts to earn their acceptance. This caused me much pain. Once I changed my model of reality, my pain went away.

My giving up the belief in power allowed me to define fewer problems and therefore produce fewer symptoms. This, in turn, leads to fewer problems with addictions. There is also one other area in which a belief in powerlessness is helpful.

Once we have defined something as a problem and decided how to feel about it, we face another choice in our map of reality. What do we do about it? I talked earlier about either treating the symptoms or solving the problem. We also have a third option. We can decide there is no need for action and let it go. We can redefine the definition we made which produced the symptoms in the first place.

If we believe we have to control things in order to be happy, it follows that we have to do something about every problem or supposed problem in our lives. On the other hand, if we believe that we do not have to control things to be happy, we can choose to do nothing, getting rid of the symptoms at the same time. This is not to say that we avoid taking action when action is necessary. It is just to say that we don't have to take action for action's sake.

This freedom of choice concerning our options under a recovery core belief is expressed well in the Serenity Prayer used in all twelve-step groups: *God, grant me the serenity to accept the things I cannot change, the courage to change the things I can, and the wisdom to know the difference.*

This prayer is for serenity, not power, for the two values are in constant competition in our minds. A choice to put one in top priority automatically precludes having the other in the same position. An acceptance of powerlessness in our lives keeps us from putting power in serenity's rightful position as the top goal in our lives. When we hold to this course, we progress in our quest for meaning.

In recovering from addictions, there is one part of this acceptance of powerlessness which must happen early. The realization that we are powerless over an addiction and our lives are unmanageable leads to the obvious. We need to remove the cause of that unmanageability from our lives. We also need to change the power-based beliefs which underlie our addictions. In order to do that, we first must start with abstaining from the addictive behavior(s) which we use to validate our false beliefs in control.

*For Your Personal Growth*

*Look at your life and review the situations you usually define as problems. What power or control over the situation do you believe you rightfully should have? Perhaps you are kicking yourself because you should have the power over yourself or better judgement. In any case, look until you identify the power you want and assess whether it is primarily security, sensation, or personal power-based.*

*Now, look at those situations again with the realization that you do not control the situations in your life. Explore how you can accept the situations you cannot change. Explore how, with the help of others, you can change some of the situations. Finally, after you have gone through these steps, ask yourself if you have developed the wisdom to know the difference between the things which you and others can change together and the things which will require intervention from a power higher than you. This is a very valuable insight.*

*Continue to work on the acceptance of situations in your life and develop a sense of gratefulness for situations which remind you that you are a part of, but not the center of, the universe.*

# ABSTINENCE

*Abstinence and the ability to have a happy life are not the same thing. As one man said, "Abstinence is like standing up at the starting line. The race hasn't started yet, but at least you are standing up rather than lying down."*

- Earnie Larsen

Each of us can best begin recovery by beginning abstinence from all power-level addictions and from all unnecessary security and sensation-level addictive behaviors. This will provide the stability needed to chip away at the rest of life. It will also prevent the failure which occurs when one merely drops one addiction and switches to other addictions in one's menu. In using the self-help group language, it is also helpful to recognize that one's life is unmanageable and will be that way as long as one does not abstain.

## Why is this Necessary?

As one of my clients pointed out, he couldn't think of any other way to know whether he had recovered than to quit. Yet addicts usually go through years of trying to control their addictions rather than practicing abstinence. This points out some controversies about whether addictions can be controlled, or whether an addict must be abstinent from his addictions. In spite of years of research and experience to the contrary, there are still those who believe it isn't necessary to abstain from addictions in order to recover. Unfortunately, some of them are health professionals.

## Abstinence Versus Control

Throughout the history of the addiction sciences, there has been this ongoing debate about whether abstinence or control should be the goal of treatment and recovery. Recent evidence comes down hard on the side of abstinence. For example, some professionals have consistently tried to teach alcoholics to control their drinking. At this stage of the research and of our clinical experience, this attempt is irresponsible, and seems to reflect the control addictions of the professionals rather than the clinical realities of alcoholism.

Whenever we encourage an addict to control his addiction, we are setting him up to progress from a sensation addiction to a power addiction. We need to avoid this at all costs.

Once an addictive behavior has progressed to the addiction level, it can't be controlled. If it can, then it isn't an addiction. In most cases, if the person attempts to control it, he will only succeed in making sure the behavior progresses to the addiction and then disease levels. In addition, such attempts are power-based and interfere with the goal of making serenity, rather than power, the top goal of recovery.

Mind you, I am not saying that persons with solely enhancement or infrequent addictive behavior patterns must abstain from those behaviors. I am referring to those persons whose addictive behaviors have reached at least the regular addictive behavior stage. All these people might benefit from abstinence, but for the persons using addictive behavior as a regular coping option, this is critical.

There are differences between truly occasional use of enhancement or addictive behavior and the regular use of such behavior to cope with life. For example, people who have not progressed to addictions to alcohol, drugs, food, or sex do not control those behaviors. They don't have the desire to abuse them! A "social drinker" doesn't want twenty-five beers in a night, at least not more often than on one, crazy night. The fact that you have ever felt a need to control a behavior in and of itself is the best indicator that you have an addiction going or developing.

## Preferences and Abstinence

In his *Handbook To Higher Consciousness*, Ken Keyes gives some very sound advice. He advises that if an addictive behavior is not necessary for survival, abstain from it. In the case of substances, it is never necessary to drink alcohol to survive. Therefore, alcoholics should quit drinking. They should do so for several reasons, one of which is that their drinking will keep them from enjoying more important things in life. Keyes also talks about upgrading addictions which are necessary for survival, such as eating, having relationships, and loving sex to "preferences."

As stated earlier, addictions are the attempts of a person to stay happy by coping with external realities by focusing on emotional states. It reflects a core belief that we can feel the way we want to feel, regardless of our problems or the level of responsibility for our behavior. In this manner, it is self-spoiling. It is also self-deluding.

Because of this, the addict in recovery should treat himself in much the same manner that a parent should treat a spoiled child whom he is trying to retrain. He should ask which of his addictive behaviors are necessary for survival, and plan on changing those behaviors from addictions to preferences. Sometimes this will be difficult. He should also decide to abstain from those addictive behaviors which are not necessary for survival, and from those parts of necessary addictive behaviors, such as eating massive amounts of sweets within food addiction, which are detrimental to him. His ability to upgrade addictions to preferences will depend greatly on whether his primary pleasure within the addiction is a security, sensation, or power-centered pleasure. He needs to look at this closely.

Looking again at an earlier example (p. 133):

| Security | Sensation | Power |
|----------|-----------|-------|
| *work* | *cocaine* | *sex* |

There are three addictions in this complex. Using the first rule of which addictions are necessary for survival, only work qualifies. The client will have to upgrade his work addiction to a preference to recover. In both of the other addictions, he needs to learn abstinence from the addictive behavior. If this does not occur, the progression will continue.

Security addictions can usually be changed to preferences. We can, for example, change from feeling a desperate need for love to preferring to be loved by certain people. We can prefer to have money, but not commit suicide if we don't. We can stop drinking to fit in with a crowd, and base the decision to drink or not to drink on other factors. We can decide to eat to survive, not survive to eat.

Mild sensation addictions can sometimes be upgraded to preferences. Sex addiction, as long is it is in the security or sensation level of progression, can be changed to a preference by most people. Eating for sensation can sometimes be changed in the same way. *As a general rule, the recommendation is to upgrade those addictions which are centered on behaviors necessary for survival to preferences, while learning to abstain from those which are not.*

This is a fine line, which should not be applied to chemical addictions. Chemicals, especially most addictive chemicals, are almost never necessary for survival.

Once an addiction has become primarily a search for power, the addict's first choice should be abstinence. This is very consistent with clinical experience, that true pedophiles and violent rapists are rarely able to return to limiting themselves to normal sexuality. It is also consistent with the accepted standard that physically addicted (powerless) alcoholics should learn to be abstinent from alcohol. Giving up the behavior is often the only way to escape the struggle a power-level addiction creates. This is true of sadomasochistic, abusive relationships, totally power-centered work addiction (he should change to a different line of work), materialism addicts who constantly abuse credit, and extreme gambling addiction in which the gambler risks becoming powerless in society or becoming injured if he loses.

The only addictions which are truly necessary for an individual's survival regardless of progression are eating and working. Everyone needs to eat, and few people do not need to work at some level to survive.

Overeaters Anonymous and other groups which help the food addict recognize the limits on the need to eat, help the overeater change preferences for which foods to eat. This is an excellent approach, but it is far more difficult for most advanced overeaters to do this than it is for most other addicts to abstain from unnecessary addictions.

Work addiction is also very insidious because the ingrained belief system is supported by almost all of society and recovery depends on a total shift of preferences which is not sanctioned by society.

**Preventing Further Progression**

Perhaps the most important reason for learning abstinence from your unneeded addictive behaviors is to prevent further progression from the current stage of the behavior to addiction and disease. In some addictive behaviors, this will almost always happen. Let's review the earlier example:

| Security | Sensation | Power |
|----------|-----------|-------|
| *work* | *cocaine* | *sex* |

In this example, there is a good likelihood that the system will shift in the near future unless abstinence from cocaine occurs immediately. The complex will probably soon look like this:

| Security | Sensation | Power |
|----------|-----------|-------|
| *work* | | *sex* |
| | | *cocaine* |

This shift will occur because of the rapidity with which cocaine users become powerless in their relationship with the drug. For this reason, the person encountering this client during the earlier pattern would have been wise to follow my proposed guidelines and recommend abstinence from cocaine while it remained at the sensation level. Further damage would have been prevented if abstinence had occurred.

## Other Considerations

In some addictions, abstinence is also necessary for physical reasons. Alcohol and drugs, for example, produce physical dependence and a physical inability to control their use. In order to even begin to think rationally, the person addicted to these substances must spend significant time in abstinence from them.

In food addiction it is impossible to abstain from all food and still survive. It is possible, however, to identify those foods which set off addictive cravings and eating patterns, and to eat other foods instead. Overeaters Anonymous and Weight Watchers are two organizations which are very good at helping people learn to change the foods they eat.

At this time there are, to my knowledge, no self-help groups for the work-addict. This presents a slight problem, but as work addicts usually have other addictions too, they can often simply apply the steps from a self-help program for another addiction to their work addiction.

## It's No Fun Anymore

Another point in abstaining from power-level addictions is that the addict can never expect to return successfully to those behaviors, without returning to the addiction. The reasons for this have nothing to do with willpower, or any other such illusion. They have to do with physical and psychological progression. Once we go so far in our addictions, they are simply no fun to practice at a less advanced level.

There have been several movies lately about this phenomena in sexual addiction. The theme of out-of-control sexuality leading to the inability to enjoy less-controlled sexual experiences is common, *and real*. I have had several cases in which a couple experimented with sexual swinging, to have the husband or wife eventually become unable to get excited without others being present. Needless to say, this created some problems with their intimacy.

As an addiction progresses from security to sensation to power levels, the person loses the ability to get any pleasure out of practicing the addiction at the previous level. He builds a psychological, and sometimes physical, tolerance. For example, when my alcoholic clients come in for diagnosis, I ask them how much alcohol it takes for them to achieve the feeling they want. We then compare their answers to blood alcohol levels they produce, and assess the security, sensation, or power levels regarding that addiction.

If a person drinks with friends, and only drinks two drinks to get his effect, he is drinking at security levels, and, if he is telling the truth, is probably not alcoholic. He is not, as common wording has it, "controlling his drinking." He simply desires to drink a small amount and does so. This is true at every level. People do not control drinking. Some people merely want more than others.

If he drinks with friends, and drinks four to six beers to get his effect, he is operating at the sensation and security levels and may or may not be alcoholic.

If he drinks with friends or alone, and drinks eight or more drinks and maintains a level well above the level of .10 blood alcohol content to get the effect he wants, he is drinking at the sensation and power/powerless levels, and needs to quit.

If you notice, the focus is on the amount it takes for the alcoholic to achieve the feeling he wants to achieve, and whether this feeling is security, sensation, or power related. The reason for this are simple. Once a person has progressed in an addiction from security to sensation or to power levels, he will not be able to enjoy addiction at the lower levels again.

If he drank for complete intoxication, there will be minimal satisfaction in drinking for a mild buzz and the addict will increase his drinking eventually to create the desired feelings of intoxication because he gets no pleasure from drinking moderately, in spite of the anticipation that he will.

There are both physical and psychological reasons for this response. Alcoholics seem to have different physical responses to alcohol than nonalcoholics. For example, they have different tolerance levels to alcohol than others have. This tolerance in most cases first climbs quite high, then later, if drinking continues, becomes very low. Another difference seems to be in how pleasureable the alcohol-affected state seems to be. The pleasure from being drunk for an alcoholic is, or at least was, very pleasureful. Both the tolerance and pleasure factors seem to be genetically related, and complement the psychological factors.

If I know a client has more than one addiction, I will explore the other addictions as well because this rule is true in all the addictions. In sex addiction, for example, once a person gets to a point where he can only get completely turned on by dominance, or group sex, or by children, he will not be able to return to casual sex and enjoy it for an extended period, without seeking the type of sex that turns him on the most. He may or not be able to experience intimate sex in a loving relationship, but that is usually a separate issue from his addictive sexuality.

Just as the alcoholic will experience an intense desire to drink, regardless of the quality of his love relationships, the sex addict will experience an intense desire for casual sex, regardless of the quality of the sexuality within his marriage or primary relationship. In extreme cases, however, it seems that any sexual relationship whatsoever will trigger urges for addictive sexuality, even the sexuality within an intimate relationship.

Work addicts tend to drive themselves to greater and greater levels of achievement in order to achieve those early feelings of power and freedom they had when they began their careers. Since work addiction and addiction to material items are complements, early work addiction has, as its foundation, fantasies of material things and power which are going to make the addict and those close to him happy. Since everyone fails to be happy as the result of the addiction, whether or not the addict achieves his goals, the work addict looks for more powerful positions from which to continue to feed self and family with possessions. He does this in order to make up for the poor emotional quality in the family. He can no longer enjoy the smaller things in life, and doesn't see how the family members are puppets to his addiction.

So you see, all addiction is a gamble, with the stakes going up as the addiction progresses. Once an addict has experienced the intensity of the power-level practice of an addiction, he will not be satisfied with playing for lower stakes.

### One-Day-At-A-Time

I need to point out that it is impossible for a power-level addict to commit to abstinence from an addiction for any long period of time. This is not to say he cannot be abstinent for long periods of time, he just can't predict that he can. The ability to be abstinent is a skill, or set of skills, he will have to learn. In the self-help groups, he learns that he can only stay abstinent "one-day-at-a-time." This is actually too long a time span for him to attack. He can only stay abstinent from his addictions in each here-and-now situation. He can stay abstinent now, but he may risk relapse this afternoon.

### Misguided Sympathy

Most of us feel sympathy for persons who must be completely abstinent from their addictive behaviors, and sometimes we help them convince themselves this is not necessary. This is extremely misguided, and may be reflective of our own denial of our inability to control our own addictions.

I have known alcoholics who died because they couldn't believe abstinence was necessary. I have also known an abused wife who was killed by a second abusive husband after leaving a first one when she created a new power-level addictive relationship. I have known several people who have filed for bankruptcy more than once because they attempted to control their use of credit. In most cases, this sympathy for the power-level addict is misguided. Abstinence from a power-centered addiction provides far more freedom for the recovering person than he would achieve by trying to continue controlling his behavior.

In fact, abstinence from unnecessary security and sensation level addictions can also offer more freedom than trying to hang on to them. We just can't know this until we upgrade them to preferences and then find we no longer prefer them.

The only addiction in which I feel sympathy for those who must stay abstinent is the sexual addicts who can only be excited by violent dimensions in their sexuality. My sympathy is for their inability to enjoy normal, loving sexuality, and our lack of a method to help them, rather than for their having to give up raping people.

While abstinence from sex is uncomfortable, sex which must entail coercion or violence to be enjoyable is simply not acceptable in civilized society. And abstinence is better than humiliating or killing others and being incarcerated or killed. For this reason, as well as many others, the more power-level addictions addicts have, the more help they need in their recovery. They need to make new friends and learn about reality. They can't do it alone.

These guidelines are hard for some addicts to accept, but usually no addict will be in a situation in which he has no historical addictions to upgrade to preferences. Those will remain sources of pleasure during his recovery, and he will be able to discover more meaningful coping methods.

**People Do Change!**

Unless we begin recovering from our addictions, we will gradually spend more and more of our time in our combined addictions, until we find another way to cope. As I have said, some of our addictions will have to be completely abandoned. Others can be "upgraded," in Keyes' terminology, to preferences. There are several factors which are relevant to the decision to abandon or upgrade an addiction.

People do move away from an addictive lifestyle. Depending on the addictive configuration, the addict will be able to slowly adopt less addictive coping, once the hangover phenomena overcome the ability to lie to self about the behavior. Once this occurs, he has "hit bottom," and is ready to begin learning other coping means.

When we are practicing addictions, we are practicing a most obvious self-delusion. We tell ourselves we receive pleasure when we don't. If we have an addiction to any behavior at a power level, we are extremely dedicated to that behavior and the inherent selfishness and dishonesty it represents. We have to shed this skin before we can grow another. The only way to begin this shedding is abstinence from any addictive behavior which is not required for survival.

*For Your Personal Growth*

*Review the addictive behaviors in your life and ask if the behaviors are necessary for your survival. Furthermore, assess whether you are at the regular addictive behavior or higher with any of the behaviors. Finally, assess whether the behavior is practiced at the security, sensation, or power levels. Make a decision to abstain from all regular addictive behaviors which are not necessary for your survival.*

*Once this decision is made, spend an hour or so a day reviewing new options during the time which was previously wrapped up in your addictions. Generate new activities which are truly loving to yourself and others. Practice this abstinence, replacing addictive behaviors with loving behaviors for three months, then review and discuss the difference in your life with someone with good recovery.*

# SPIRITUALITY

*I believe that sobriety, process, and spirituality are all words for the same process.*

- Anne Wilson-Schaef

Spirituality is the primary key to the success of all the twelve-step programs. This is not just my opinion, but the opinion of almost every successfully recovering person I have ever known. Both the second and third steps refer to coming to believe that a "power greater than ourselves could restore us to sanity," and making a decision to "turn our will and our lives over to the care of God as we understood Him." Most of the people who fail in recovery do so, not because they can't face quitting their addictions, but because they can't come to terms with their spiritual needs.

When I first encountered this position about spirituality among AA members, I felt insulted. I was well-trained in counseling theory and technique and felt that my skill was being demeaned when others told me that no one could hope to help an addicted person without dealing with the issues of spirituality in his life. This feeling of outrage, which I have outgrown as a result of experience, is shared today by many members of the helping professions. This is unfortunate. The "Void" is a spiritual, not a mental, issue and cannot be analyzed away.

Spirituality means something different in each of our minds. This is very ingrained in our personal maps of reality and we have strong opinions about it. We all have personal ideas about God's existence or non-existence and what God means to us. In this book, spirituality refers to one's perception of self in relation to the universe and other beings in it. This is a very broad reference, and is relevant for persons of all religions.

Many recovering people fear both God and other human beings. This is the result of problems in their models of reality which often develop in their families. When they face entering the family of a recovery group, they do so with expectations of the rejection and pain they have experienced before. When this doesn't happen, this softens their rigidity in trusting larger aspects of their environments. When we are there for others in recovery, we literally become interpreters for our Higher Power. We do this by presenting to them the type of loving acceptance which we feel is appropriate to share with our brothers and sisters. What we do is the message.

## Our God Image

As M. Scott Peck pointed out in *The Road Less Traveled,* many of us have images of God as a very critical being. Some of our images are so critical that our ideas of God and Satan are so alike that we often prefer our Satan image. We, according to Peck, learn these images due to the interaction we have with parents and other adults when quite young. The more critical your environment, the more likely you are to have an unfavorable impression of God. If you received only conditional love you will tend to view God's love as the most conditional of all. He also states that all therapy has at its core, a resolution of this concern with the lovingness or hostility of the universe.

This is very consistent with my experience. Many of my clients are agnostic when entering treatment. They may have been raised in religious homes, in fact many of them were, but they have very negative perceptions of God. The idea of spirituality is very hard for them to accept and this retards their recovery. Most of the time, they have to be lead through the experience of unconditional acceptance to slowly develop a spiritual awareness.

## Mortality

One of the reasons spirituality is so difficult for us is that our bodies are mortal and our model of reality is that we are our bodies. Spiritual models tell us that we are more than bodies, and that the important part of what we are is immortal. If we have no spiritual model and haven't come to grips with physical mortality, we are often obsessed with death and fear it greatly. This prevents us from learning to love because too much of our energy is taken up fearing death. Even when we love, we will begin to create "Void" feelings by worrying about the deaths of our love objects. This flips us right back into wanting to change our feelings, because we believe this is a problem which has no solution.

A very sad thing occurs when someone spends most of the time obsessed with fear of death. His emotional/spiritual self can never completely live. The fear of a physical death creates an emotional death. Addicts often have a very difficult time getting out of this rut. They defend the assault on their health, the damage caused by their addictions, by stating they are going to die anyway, so leave them alone. This relates to the unresolved fear of death and the lack of a spiritual component in their maps of reality.

## Who Controls?

Throughout the book, I have argued that a conflict in addiction is between powerlessness and self-control. In spiritual terms, the question for the addict is whether he controls reality or a higher power controls it. For the addict in denial, the very idea that he might not be in control is often terrifying. Accepting the idea of outside control, or of there being no need for control, represents a major movement forward in maturity.

The higher levels of Hall's stages of consciousness, as well as Erikson's stages of development, are very concerned with spirituality and the practice of spiritual values. The higher levels, which we want to achieve eventually, see the world as a project to improve. We all have to maximize the sense that we fit in and belong to creation if we are to experience the peace of mind the recovery programs call serenity.

If you are trying to recover from an addiction, pursue a spiritual recovery program. Start with a twelve-step program, even if you are an active church member. You do not need to change from a church spiritual program to a self-help program, but you can still add the self-help group to your life. The reasons for this are simple.

At times during this process, you will experience the direct opposite of what I have termed *"rational madness."* You will experience moments of *"irrational sanity,"* in which you simply know you are on the right track, in spite of the fact you have no data to prove it. Recovering people in spiritual programs become very aware reality is not always "rational" on the surface. They become very comfortable with waiting for the underlying rationality of a new behavior or insight to reveal itself. Anne Wilson-Schaef terms this "living in process." It is a necessary skill.

The twelve steps and self-help groups offer unconditional acceptance to addicted persons. Churches often do not. Furthermore, the ignorance about addictions in most church groups tends to set up a dynamic in which you can only be a good member if you abstain *successfully* from your addictions. In the self-help groups, you only have to *desire* to abstain. They recognize the day-at-a-time nature of recovery, and put no conditions on their members except for the desire to recover. For this reason, they work better.

Spirituality exists at two levels: that of the spiritual exchange in fellowship with others and that of the process of turning one's life over to the care of God as we understand Him. When this is explored in self-help groups, it provides the recovering person with a means of connecting with his fellow, addicted humans and with the universe. This seems to be necessary to counteract the emotional isolation of addiction.

It also settles the question of who controls your life. If you are turning your life over to the care and direction of God, you are further accepting the powerlessness we explored in the last chapter. You are also committing to a spiritual relationship. The biggest difficulty most of us have with this step is taking back the power. During early recovery, we know that our addictions aren't working, but we don't accept that our coping decisions are breaking our hearts. When we first begin recovery, we are willing to turn over the care and direction of our lives to anyone. When we feel better as the result of doing so, however, we immediately want the control back. This sabotages our recovery and our serenity.

### "He Doesn't Do It Right"

Jackie was a very attractive young lady who first consulted me due to problems with shoplifting. As we completed her intake, it was obvious that the shoplifting was only one dimension of a gambling addiction. She bet on races and sports and liked to go to Las Vegas. She also had a history of setting herself up with abusive males. She worked obsessively to feed her addiction; the relationship she was in at the time was definitely addictive.

When she first started therapy, she was willing to do anything. She had committed her third offense and was facing jail time. She began attending a twelve-step program and group and individual therapy at our clinic. At first she was very successful.

Jackie very rapidly developed problems, however, with one part of the program. She couldn't follow their advice to avoid new relationships for a year. Her boyfriend left when she no longer gambled with him, and she was left without a man. This set off withdrawals, and she immediately began looking. When she shared her new exploits with me, I confronted her about going back to running her own life rather than turning it over to God. Her response was, "But, He doesn't do it right! It's been two months since Roger left. I'm getting tired of being lonely." Within a month of that conversation, Jackie was caught shoplifting again. She stole a shirt for a new boyfriend. She went to jail for thirty days for that one, but has since done very well at "turning it over."

When children of God show love to someone, it is easier for that person to believe that God is loving. So the spiritual connections for recovering addicts start with the loving relationships they develop with each other. This "spirit" of love allows for higher connections. I encourage you to put a great deal of time and effort into understanding just where you fit in the universe. You do fit, whether you know it or not. Learn how to turn it over to God, however you define God. The benefits of this time and effort will be worth it.

*For Your Personal Growth*

*Read the following instructions, then close your eyes and do the exercise.*

*Go inside yourself and get in touch with your feelings and image of God. Pull together as much detail as possible. Now pay attention to your feelings about that image. Open your eyes and remember the impression.*

*Now, go inside and get in touch with your feelings and image of evil or Satan. Again, pull together as much detail as possible. Now pay attention to your feelings about that image.*

*Finally, compare the two images and the feelings you have about them. Which image holds the most attraction for you? With which one do you feel most comfortable?*

*Remember this exercise as you ask yourself whether your images were appropriate and where you picked up the images and feelings you discovered. Finally, share this exercise with someone else.*

*Once this sharing is completed, seek out someone you know who seems to be very calm and serene. Ask that person how they perceive these two images. Compare his or her image to yours and see what you learn.*

# THROWING OUT THE GARBAGE

*Love and guilt cannot coexist,*
*and to accept one is to deny the other.*
- A Course In Miracles

Once we are well-grounded in the spiritual aspects of a twelve-step program, we begin to advance within that spirituality to healing the concrete damage addiction has caused in our lives and in the lives of those around us. We identify things in ourselves which need changing, including our self-centeredness, and set out to make those changes. We also identify how these things have affected our relationships with others and make attempts to heal these relationships. This is a process of sorting through and throwing out our emotional garbage.

Years ago, when I worked in a local inpatient alcoholism center, one of the other therapists did a lecture about feelings. He used the metaphor of storing trash in a garbage can in the summer with the top on and leaving it out in the sun. He pointed out that if we did that, the light and heat of the sun would eventually result in the chemical action of the garbage blowing the lid off the can, releasing a very powerful stench.

Likewise, when we store up garbage feelings in ourselves, it is only a matter of time before, under the illumination of contact with others, the internal interactions of these feelings will cause us to explode and reveal stinking behavior and feelings. Whether we are dealing with the trash from our homes, or with the trashy feelings inside us, it is necessary to regularly *throw out the garbage*.

There are steps by which we can accomplish this in a twelve-step program.

In the twelve-step programs of recovery, there is the concept in the fourth step of a "fearless and searching moral inventory." The idea is that, once someone has decided that he can't handle an addiction, and has made the appropriate spiritual commitments, he needs to identify just where he is in life. This is a way of looking at his addictive map of reality and evaluating it to see what he needs to change.

After he completes this inventory, the addict is to share with God and another human being the results of the inventory. Following that, he is to make a list of all the people to whom he owes amends for behavior for which he is ashamed. Then, he is to actually make amends to those people, when such action would create no harm to self or others. Finally, he is to continue to take these inventories, and when wrong about something, promptly admit it.

### The Law of Karma

In most spiritual systems, there is a notion that "what goes around comes around." The previously mentioned steps address this idea. When we are living addictively, our self-centered view of reality makes it inevitable that we will hurt people unnecessarily. When we can't recognize that others have equally valid needs as we do, we can't respect those needs. Addictions blind us to the needs of others and also lead us to devalue our obligation to treat others the way we would like to be treated.

After several years of this perspective, it is likely that we have wronged several people. We know it, and when we quit treating the guilt and shame from such behavior with addictive behavior, it hurts to know it. The "fourth step inventory" is a way of looking at all this guilt and shame, and seeing it as one price we have paid for our addiction. It is also, however, a means of giving ourselves the potential for getting rid of these negative feelings.

When we are honest with ourselves about our deficiencies, we increase the possibility of self-improvement. When we share it with someone else, and that person accepts us anyway, we move toward trust. When we share it with God and don't get struck down by lightning, we even begin to trust Him. Finally, when we approach someone we have wronged, make amends to that person, and have him accept those amends, it dramatically reduces the guilt and shame of our previous behavior.

Earlier, I defined addiction as a coping style in which one treated feelings with addictive behavior. The more severe the feelings of guilt and shame an addict has, the higher the risk of relapse. Getting rid of negative feelings reduces this risk. It is well worth the pain.

## Unrealistic Self-Image

Another aspect of this garbage-dumping and amends-making is the discovery of hidden treasures. In doing a moral inventory, we also discover some things about ourselves which aren't so bad. We have to look at our bad points *and* our good points.

Sometimes we discover these treasures during the amends-making process. We start to apologize for awful behavior only to find that the other person didn't find it awful at all. We also discover who values us enough to love us with all our faults.

Addiction produces distortions in our images of ourselves. Between the self-centeredness of our world model and the experience that many of us had of overly critical family systems, it is difficult to have accurate self-perceptions. This inventory process forces us to look at ourselves in new ways and to share these new perceptions with others. This is a valuable process.

## Forgiveness

I have already stated that spirituality is an essential element of recovery from addiction. I would like to state now that forgiveness is the action through which we express that spirituality and our love. It is the master key to serenity. Unfortunately, its importance is often overlooked.

There are three aspects to forgiveness. First, we forgive ourselves for our imperfections. Second, we forgive others for things which have occurred which have permanently harmed us.

There will be very few of these things to forgive. Third, we give up the illusion that anyone else has harmed us by not catering to our security, sensation, and power addictions. The first two aspects have to do with removal of old emotional baggage. The third has to do with not accumulating emotional garbage in the first place. This third aspect is the most liberating.

First, however, we need to deal with the forgiveness of ourselves. The process of an inventory, sharing, and making amends allows us to get started. Once we begin to see ourselves as worthy of love and forgiveness, we can begin to see others in the same way. This is difficult to achieve unless we have first explored our spirituality and developed a feeling of connection with a Higher Power as a result of that exploration.

Second, we may have suffered permanent damage as the result of the actions of someone else. We may be handicapped, or scarred for life in some other way, from some incident in our history. Forgiveness of those who may have been responsible removes a block to wholly accepting our fellow human beings. To hold on to anger separates us from those we would love and who would love us. For this reason, we need to forgive, to let go of the stored up garbage of our anger. We can't change the past. When we dredge it up as an angry feeling, we prevent ourselves from enjoying the now.

Finally, we need to give up our illusions of being harmed by the actions of others when they are only guilty of frustrating our desires for security, sensation, and power. This is a major tool in being able to maintain serenity now. Any moment that we are judging someone else in an angry manner is a moment in which we forfeit our serenity.

For example, I want you to remember someone you still feel angry with for something he or she has done. Remember, in detail, the situation and exactly why you were angry. Now, ask yourself how you are still damaged today by his or her action. If you are not damaged today, I bet that all that person did was refuse to cater to your idea of how you should be treated. He or she didn't support your addictive demands. Forgiving that person consists of admitting to yourself that you weren't truly harmed in the first place.

In most cases, when we do this exercise, we can look closer and even see a way in which our lives are better today because the person did what we didn't like. Instead of feeling grateful for the lesson we learned, however, we are busy holding on to angry feelings for a spiritual brother, sister, or a parent.

Taking this a step further, we need to learn to deal with ongoing situations with the same frame of mind. Almost every situation in your life in which you are angry or unhappy, is linked to your emotionally demanding that you get your way and judging that you are being damaged when you don't. Ken Keyes refers to this when he defines addictions as "emotion-backed demands for security, sensations, and/or power." To counter these feelings which tend to isolate us from others, we need to learn to forgive instantly, recognizing that not getting our way does not damage us.

The next time you are driving and become angry at another driver, ask yourself how this person is harming you and if the feelings you are creating are worth foregoing your primary goal of maintaining serenity. See if you can determine whether you are feeling a threat to your feelings of security, sensations, or power. Then, let go of the illusion that this person is causing your angry feelings. You are creating them through your interpretation of the situation.

Now, turn this exercise inward on yourself. Look for situations in your life over which you feel guilt or shame. How many of those situations are ones where you were only "guilty" of frustrating someone else's addictions. Most family-induced shame results from this pattern.

The child who feels guilt because she was never the child her mother wanted feels guilty because she was criticized for not being able to cater to her mother's power addictions. This guilt serves no purpose whatsoever. The later step in the twelve-step program, of promptly admitting when we are wrong, is the only appropriate response to guilt, as long as we are attempting to be loving people.

Except for the positive purpose of providing motivation for making immediate amends for self-centered behavior, guilt is a perfectly worthless emotion. It interferes with serenity and is a waste of time. So you made a mistake yesterday, so what? If you harmed someone, you have amends to make. In any case, feeling guilt today prevents you from being serene today. In this sense, feeling guilty is a way of making the same mistake twice. Yesterday I messed up. Today I do the same thing in a new way by feeling guilty about it.

Forgiveness is a powerful, necessary skill in recovery. By forgiving ourselves and others, we keep our lives free from addictive conflicts. We also change our interpersonal ideas of victimization. This is very important too.

We are not the victims of the world we see. We are, instead, the co-creators of that world, along with all the other people in our lives. We do this creating within the influence of the culture at large, and are unable to fully comprehend the effect of that culture. We attract the other co-creators to us, and keep them in our lives, precisely because they reinforce our views and, if we have them, our addictions.

We maintain our feelings of being victims by interpreting situations so as to convince ourselves we are under attack when we don't get our way. Forgiveness in this final context is only refusing to participate in this illusion-building.

In this chapter, we have covered getting rid of emotional garbage through an inventory, sharing, and amends-making process. We also have covered a second level of forgiving ourselves and others for past wrongs which have resulted in permanent damage. Finally, I have presented a model for preventing ourselves from creating emotional garbage in the first place. Together, these are effective tools for change. You will need to practice using these tools in relationships with others, the topic of the next chapter.

*For Your Personal Growth*

*Practice the exercise outlined in this chapter in your interactions with others.*

*Also, practice recognizing when others are creating negative feelings by becoming upset when their emotion-backed demands for security, sensation, and power aren't catered to. Don't try to teach them differently. Just watch them. They will teach you much about yourself.*

# LEARNING FROM OTHERS

*We are not the victims of the world we see.*
- A Course In Miracles

The previous three chapters have outlined principles of recovery from addictions which are consistent with the twelve steps used in self-help groups. Just understanding the ideas themselves, however, isn't nearly enough to ensure recovery. The previous concepts need to be supported within groups of other recovering people. There are critical recovery skills which *can only* develop in interactions with others. A person may be able to abstain from an addiction alone, but he will need the help of others to develop the serenity necessary to maintain this new life-style.

Early recovery should center on peer learning in communal self-help and treatment environments. There are many crucial skills learned at this time. Two of the most important are responsibility, the ability to respond appropriately to problems, and self-esteem, the ability to maintain a consistent image of one's self as being valuable. This learning process requires that the recovering person become a member of a group of people who can teach and model those skills. This is very difficult for addicts because they have always viewed themselves as victims in previous family and work groups. Their "victim viewpoint" prevents them from feeling comfortable in non-addictive groups. This perception is deadly.

## Victim Consciousness

Everyone who maintains destructive addictions has, as a cornerstone of his illusions, the belief that he is a *victim* of the world and of his addictive complements. He perceives himself as operating within the options defined by others and denies his attempts to restrict their options. In order for him to recover from addictions, this is a perspective which must change. Feeling like a victim can be lethal for an addict.

Whenever you find yourself feeling like a victim, you are probably judging someone for frustrating an emotional demand. When feeling persecuted by someone, you gain some perverse sense of meaning and drama out of being in the morally superior position. This is dangerous. But anyone who has tried to talk a battered wife into leaving her husband knows the power of this part of addiction. In any conflict, we can focus on being a victim or focus on improving things as soon as possible. Only the second option is healthy.

Another approach to relationships which prevents the addict from learning from others is the belief that his role is to *rescue* others in relationships. This is an emotional demand for power in a sneaky, very destructive form. This rescuer role may be the closest to a positive style an addict will experience in his family of origin. If that is true, this is the most positive role in his model of reality and the model needs to be expanded. Rescuers create immaturity in those around them.

The third approach is that of *persecutor*. All members of addictive families develop the ability to treat other members very cruelly. I made the case earlier that they are all addicts or addicts-in-training, and they all learn the persecutor role. A practicing addict tends to persecute people. When he is abstaining and not in recovery, he tends to protect or rescue those same people. The major dramas that occur in the addictive family are dramas played out between victims, rescuers, and persecutors. If a member of this family wants to break out of this pattern, he will need to learn from someone outside his family.

This three-role universe was first pointed out by practitioners of Transactional Analysis in the early seventies. The addict tends to give up persecuting in early recovery, but will approach his joining a group in a rescuer manner whenever possible, and will surround himself with others who will let him rescue. This is inappropriate, as his role should be that of a student, learning from others who are more advanced in recovery. This rescuer myth, however, is well-grounded in our cultural mythology and hard to give up.

If you want to be happy in life, it is a necessary, common-sense reality that you need to be surrounded by people who are about as happy as you are, or who are more happy than you. It is amazing to me how many people believe the opposite. Most addictive people believe that they can be happy by surrounding themselves with people who "need them," or whom they need, in a childlike manner. This is a prescription for drama, but not happiness.

When we surround ourselves with people to rescue, we often do so because we feel inadequate and need the constant comparison to unfortunates for distraction from our own inadequate feelings. Both victim and rescuer feelings are usually a distortion of reality.

In a society which teaches false ways to be happy in the first place, the belief that we can be happy by surrounding ourselves with those who need us for their survival is like believing we can climb a mountain carrying four paraplegics on our backs better than with four self-sufficient, athletic people who can pull an equal weight. This is an insane belief and, when one practices it in relationships, he becomes as emotionally and physically exhausted as someone who tries to carry four others up a mountain.

Each person needs to carry his own weight in life, and not to do so is to remain a spoiled child. Addiction is a coping strategy which maintains the self-deception of not being expected to carry one's own weight. Naturally, the outcome of this behavior is less competence in the area of the addiction, and unhappiness in general. Addicts are usually involved in several relationships with people who don't want to carry their own weight either. They respond to those people by alternately feeling like their victim, persecutor, or rescuer.

In order to learn to live a happy life, you need happy people to learn from. We co-create our models of reality with others and we are all vulnerable to peer pressure. When we are members of a group, that group will mirror back to us our model of reality and that model will change slowly, based on their feedback.

If we surround ourselves with unhappy people, they will mirror back those parts of our models of reality which keep them unhappy. We will, in this interaction, add to our repertoire of ways to be unhappy. It isn't smart to involve ourselves in these situations often, if at all.

I was once attacked by a supervisor because I didn't do something I didn't know how to do or even that I was supposed to do. When I tried to explain, he attacked me again for making excuses, and right in the middle of the chaos, I came to a conclusion and answered back in a very confident voice, "Ignorance is not an excuse; it is a reason." This quieted my supervisor and has quieted my criticism of others ever since. Since people do not know that they need to surround themselves with happy people in order to be happy, anyone attacking them for this ignorance is being cruel.

This principle of needing happy people is simple. So, now that you know the principle, you need to put it into practice. Before you add new people to your life, assess whether they will add to the happy, loving parts of your life, or to the heavy, dramatic parts. Choose your friends from those in the first category.

Given that our society teaches addiction, we need to be very careful in the beginning searches for happy people to train us to be happy. As this book is about addictions, the first place to look for those people is in self-help groups for people who have recovered and who are recovering from the same addictions. People in these groups also need to surround themselves with happy people and they know it. They will teach others to be happy too, not because they are failures and they need to surround themselves with failures, but because once we are successful at learning to be happy, we can help keep others from falling back into their unhappy ways. This is really the way any truly happy person will initially approach someone who wants to learn from him, but it is also the central group ethic in self-help groups.

Even within these self-help groups, you need to use some discretion in your choice of whom to ask for help. There are many pilgrims in these groups, and most new members are initially attracted to several who are little, if any, happier than themselves. These are not the people from which they have a great deal to learn. They are fellow pilgrims, but not teachers. You need, however, to be cautious and stay away from those who seem to need you to become involved in an addiction with them, especially a sex or relationship addiction. They can be dangerous.

The people to look for to teach you, are those who use a minimum of descriptions of themselves, or of others, as victims. They will not put up with your descriptions of your addictions as justified, and will be hard on you at times about this dishonesty. Most people in self-help groups have been dealing with their addictions for several years, and have knowledge of thinking and interpersonal skills you need if you are to be successful.

In other areas of life, we can find people who are happy and with whom we can have close friendships. We need these people too. They can add variety to our lives, because we will be forced to connect with them on some basis other than our addictions. In these relationships, we discover lovable parts of ourselves we didn't dream existed.

It is your responsibility to create a group of people for yourself in which the peer pressure is to be happy, and to be responsible for yourself. Because only a small percentage of people in our culture know that they aren't victims, the creation of this group will be a time-consuming and gradual process. By starting with self-help groups, you can get a jump on things and speed the process drastically. You are also responsible for approaching these groups with the understanding that we all have much to teach each other about happiness. You can't be a victim in this group and be happy at the same time.

## The Twelve Steps

In virtually all the self-help groups, there is a list of twelve steps which we are to follow in order to develop a happy life. These steps have been used by millions in the successful attempts to build happy lives. Unfortunately, many people who enter self-help groups don't follow those steps because the steps fail to make sense in their addictive model of reality. These people usually fail in their attempts to deal with their addictions and to be happy.

If you go to a self-help group and find that you believe the twelve steps are strange, remember that millions have successfully used them to be happy. If you don't know a great deal about being happy, any system that can lead you in that direction will be foreign to your internal experience. Your inability to understand the twelve steps may be the most obvious evidence that you need to follow them. Follow them. They work.

## Group Pathology

I want to reinforce the importance of learning to protect yourself from the pathology of groups. There are many groups which actively promote addictive behavior and there are persons in self-help groups who will sabotage your attempts at growth due to their own pathology. You can expect pressure to relapse from either one of these sources.

When I constantly hear in the media that "peer pressure" is the main reason teenagers give for their drug use, I don't know whether to laugh or cry. The problem with this statement is the implication that this is only a problem for teenagers. The major reason any of us live addictive life-styles is because neither we nor our peers know any better way to live. This is even more true of adults than of teen-agers, but we act as if peer pressure is something which magically appears at about the time of puberty and goes away in our twenties. This is not true. The addictions of our peers may not pressure us into developing the same addictions, but we will always feel pressure to participate in addictive coping as long as our peers cope in this manner.

From the experience with German genocide in World War II, to the Mylai massacre in Vietnam, to the Manson murders, to the Jonestown Massacre, (all examples of out-of-control power/powerless addictions) history has given us countless instances of decent human beings following peer pressure to destroy themselves and others. We can't begin to consider all the ways a group can create a jointly insane model of reality and then convince its members that behavior which would be considered insane by anyone outside of that group is quite rational.

Our society is addictive enough, but within the society are several groups who sincerely believe that addictive coping is the only way to cope. The most obvious place to find such a group is at your friendly neighborhood bar. The regulars at this institution will be fanatics about the rationality of drinking as a coping model. Stay away from those people, even if your addiction isn't alcohol. If you spend too much time around them, you will think your addiction is rational too.

One group even exists which promotes the concept that pedophilia is good for the children who are seduced and raped by pedophiles. This group has many members and has the purpose of making insane, sexually addictive behavior seem rational.

Any group which is to truly help us beat any addiction must be very clear that we were protagonists, not victims, in our addictive process. It was our decision to cope with life by involving ourselves with another relationship addict or by practicing addictive behavior which made us unhappy. If we fail to face this fact in any way, we will try addictive coping again. This will slow our recovery and create needless pain.

## Changing Groups

People wanting to deal with addictions have little choice but to drop out of the groups which reinforce those addictions. They also need to avoid loneliness by joining and building new groups which reinforce their abstinence. This should be done as rapidly as possible.

Most people think this is simple, but it isn't. In some communities, for example, there are no self-help groups, even for alcoholics. Alcoholics Anonymous is a large organization, but self-help groups for other addictions are not yet very large and lack meetings even in some large metropolitan areas. People in less populated areas probably should seek out a therapist who specializes in addictive behaviors, including the ones causing them problems. Be careful, however, that this therapist is dealing with his own addictions before you ask for help with yours.

It is difficult to find and create new support groups but it must be done. After someone has been in therapy long enough to have some stability, he can become involved in starting a self-help group for himself and other addicts in his area. This is a good way of taking responsibility for creating his own support.

Another difficult issue is the issue of quitting an existing addictive group. While it is imperative that we remove ourselves from groups which reinforce our addictions, this is not easy and may be complicated. All our friends and our spouse's friends may be in an addictive group. Our children may play with their children. If we want to drop this group we will receive family pressure to stay in it. If this pressure is too great we need to find a therapist and ask for help with this issue.

Often the issue of leaving a group is less important than how to leave it. The answer is simple. Run! Avoid seeking out members of the group and trying to explain, especially if they are not alone. Even if they are alone, they won't be able to be very supportive. The reasons for this are simple.

Any time a member of a group leaves because the group values do not fit his needs anymore, his actions are experienced as an insult to the value system of each loyal member of that group. We need to understand this, because when we decide to leave a group, we may be psychologically attacked. This may occur for two reasons.

First, if the purpose of the group is to maintain the illusions inherent in an addiction, our leaving automatically confronts the denial of each member's addictions. Our recovery is an example of something they need to do, and as such it feels like an attack.

Second, we are choosing to distance ourselves from those who consider themselves our friends. Our leaving will produce feelings of grief, because the relationships between addicts in a group are themselves symbiotic and parts of those relationships may be loving. They will try to keep us in the group to avoid their grief.

We need to get out of our addictive groups as quickly and cleanly as possible and stay out of their gathering places. We need to forget false bravery because addictive groups are a threat to our happiness. We can let individual members seek us out and explain to them on our own turf. In that way, we find out which of them are really friends.

We need the help of others to give up addictive behavior. The sooner we realize this and act on the realization, the sooner we will learn to live a happy life. We can enlist others in our cause of creating a workable model of reality as soon as possible and we will benefit greatly from doing so. The improvement in our lives which occurs by no longer having to carry other addicts is great. The finding of fellow travelers who can work with us on our journey is greater still.

If you have been abstinent from your primary addiction(s) for six months, begin to explore recovery from the rest of the addictions in your complex. I feel that you will do best if you work toward abstinence from addictive coping within two years of quitting your power-level addictions.

Finally, learn to play in healthy ways. We have an amazing ability to create new ruts once we have left old ones behind. Too many recovering people simply quit playing and recreating once they give up the addictive manners of doing so. This is boring and unnecessary and threatens recovery.

We all deserve to enjoy life to our fullest capacity. A person in recovery has a capacity to enjoy life and recreation to a far greater degree than one who is living addictively. Furthermore, newly recovering people need to see us enjoying ourselves! Get on with it. The rest of us need playmates.

I hope this chapter has helped you understand that life can and will be better after recovery from addictive coping if we involve ourselves with others in making it so. The recovering people I know are far happier, on the average, than others in our society. It is as though the years of interfering with their own joy have motivated them to enjoy the current years more. I encourage you, again, to get to know these people and to enjoy yourself too.

*For Your Personal Growth*

*Take a good look at your friends and family and evaluate which ones play rescuers, victims, and persecutors. Whom do you rescue consistently? Who persecutes you? Whom do you feel you have to help?*

*Talk to someone you are sure has a different addiction than yours about that addiction. Explore how he and his friends comprehend their choices about the behavior. See how these arguments parallel your addictive logic.*

*If you feel you have an addiction, attend some open self-help groups and see how the descriptions of their experience of addiction parallel yours. Look for similarities, not differences.*

*Talk to a person who has been in recovery for some time and compare and contrast his life to that of the addicted person you interviewed earlier. What did you learn?*

# ADVANCED RECOVERY

*Don't aim at success - the more you aim at it and make it a target, the more you are going to miss it. For success, like happiness, cannot be pursued; it must ensue, and it only does so as the unintended side-effect of one's personal dedication to a cause greater than oneself or as the by-product of one's surrender to a person other than oneself. Happiness must happen, and the same holds for success; you have to let it happen by not caring about it.*

- Viktor E. Frankl

Once you have followed the early recovery steps outlined so far, you will have at least returned to the starting point in your quest for meaning in your life. Returning to the metaphor of the trip, you have stopped going towards Boston and have returned to Chicago on your way to San Diego. You will not return to the exact starting point. Instead, you will be taking the most direct path from the point at which you started recovery to your destination. This is efficient, as long as you do not stop at this point. The most exciting part of the journey lies ahead.

This stage of your travels has been termed "Stage II Recovery" by Earnie Larsen. This is a very good way to describe it. The tendency of most addicts is to become stable in their recovery with a few new friends and one or two self-help groups which they attend regularly. They fall short of *practicing the principles in all their affairs* and set themselves up for problems later. One way to avoid this is to continue the higher recovery steps and continue to develop new skills of personal development.

Just as Stage I Recovery has some tasks, Stage II Recovery has tasks which build upon the previous ones. Those tasks are:

*1. Develop, over time, a different model of reality, which is rational, flexible, and loving, and which has a sense of "coherence."*

*2. Practice living within this new model of reality, with the help of others who love you, who can validate your new coping decisions and offer feedback when you return to the old coping model.*

*3. Gradually replace all the old addictive behaviors and feelings, with new ones which are loving and add to the total happiness of self and others.*

*4. Completely integrate the core belief that happiness is something which results from the love returned from those whom one loves without reservation or condition, from the emotional acceptance of one's beauty, capability, and lovability, and from the acceptance of, and gratefulness for, one's actual place in the universe.*

This last belief reflects a high level of emotional and spiritual maturity. This integration of beliefs is your developmental destination, your San Diego. The other recovery steps are merely that, steps on your journey.

Any successful model of personal change is successful because it helps build models of reality that work better than the previous ones. If a method of change doesn't result in more effective modeling and coping, then it won't work. As stated in The Introduction, this is one model of addictions, not the only model of addictions. The intent is that this model, by allowing for broader understanding, will help most people with addictions live happier lives. My experience indicates that the model does indeed work.

**A Sense of Coherence**

I have used the term "coherence" throughout the book to describe the central feeling that the world is predictable and makes sense. This ability to help us understand and predict the world seems to be the essence of successful models. In addition to this model, some of you will find other models that work for you. We all can benefit by continuing to study and explore better ways of coping.

When one functions within survival consciousness, the world is confusing and incoherent. In order for people to be successful in dealing with one or more addictions, they must change the model of reality in which the insane behavior of addictive coping seems sane. They must develop a new model of reality which offers them a chance to have a high degree of happiness, and which assures them that their world has "coherence," that it "makes sense."

No matter how an addict approaches recovery, the outcome of his approach needs to be the development of a new model of reality, including a model for a different coping style. He should also work toward models which other addicts have used successfully. In my experience, any successful model of reality must at least be rational, flexible, and loving. The further we progress in our development, the more we are capable of operating in a rational, flexible, and loving manner.

I stated, in "Control, Powerlessness and Addiction," we use three mechanisms to maintain consistency in our models of reality. We delete information which does not fit. We also distort information so that it does fit. Finally, we generalize data to make it unimportant to us.

In creating a new model of reality, or in making positive modifications to an existing one, one needs to do the opposite of what serves to maintain consistency in the old model. In this way one becomes open to learning new skills and identity.

We need to do three things with new data in order for it to have an effect on our models of reality. We need to include new data which has been useful to others in similar situations. We need to clarify that data to make sure that we understand it accurately. Finally, we need to specify the usefulness of the data to us. Although people find this process difficult, and it is, the task is eased when we surround ourselves with others who can tell whether we are succeeding or failing. You can build a better, more accurate model of reality if you follow the above steps.

I have studied several systems of therapy, spirituality, and personal growth in hopes of developing a better model that I could share with others. There have been many hours of sharing with recovering people discussing the elements of their success. The ideas presented here represent a synthesis of these experiences and studies, and, as such, are a model of other models.

I have already exposed my bias that addicts should use self-help groups for recovery and involve themselves with healthy human beings. I would like to reinforce that idea, and add some other considerations for those of you who really want happier lives. Those considerations are the skills of honest, unconditional loving, and of competence in our decision-making as we cope with reality.

## Honesty

All the twelve-step programs tell us that we have to develop the ability to live a life that is rigidly honest. The fastest way for an addictive person to move in the direction of relapse is to lie, in words or actions. The most effective way to progress in recovery is to always tell the truth to self and others. Truth is the only weapon we have against addiction. Vigilance is required to prevent being hypnotized by confusion. The quickest way to become confused is to lie or to leave a lie unchallenged in your consciousness. Practice the skill of telling the truth in all things. This is the only way for you and those around you to know the truth.

## Unconditional Loving

I often see clients who have been sober from alcoholism for years, but who are in crisis because others are unhappy with their performance in relationships. The relationship addictions were never addressed, and the co-addict has outgrown the mutual addiction. In order to counter this, the recovering person needs to learn to be loving to himself and to those who are important to him.

If you are in recovery and in a relationship, address the relationship issues as soon as your therapist feels you can. Make no major decisions right away, but don't let your relationship go without attention for more than a year after quitting your other addiction(s). Learning to love yourself and then love others in the same manner is a critical set of skills.

I believe that a person's capability for unconditionally loving self and others establishes broad or narrow limits to the happiness and serenity that can be achieved. I agree with Earnie Larsen when he states:

> *I believe that learning to make relationships work is at the core of recovery....Doing so takes skill, and skills are learned. People may "feel" love but the reality of love is lived out in the context of a relationship, or it remains just a feeling.*

This focus on unconditional love is the direct opposite of addictive thinking, which states that one's happiness depends upon the degree to which he can get *others* to love him. This is a position which leaves me open to many questions, but my experience convinces me that unconditional love is fundamental to recovery from an addictive life-style. When we practice unconditional love, we are practicing skills which normally occur only at advanced levels of maturity. This serves to increase our momentum in moving along our developmental paths.

Earlier in the book, I discussed the "Void," or "black hole" feeling that we often have before we begin our addictive behavior. This feeling exists, not because we aren't loved, but rather it exists because we don't know how to love. As the result of not knowing how to love, our relationships with others are unpredictable and feel unsafe to us, regardless of how others feel towards us. We may or may not be loved, but it doesn't matter, because we are so confused about love that we can't recognize it anyway. This occurs for several reasons.

One of the reasons it occurs is our cultural belief that love is something we earn. Many believe they must be good to be loved. If this is true, and it isn't, we must do something to get someone to love us. That means, we have to operate on a power level and try to manipulate someone to love us. It also means we are not lovable unless we jump through some imaginary hoops. Since real love exists as the next level of interaction above addictive levels of human strategies, we become confused by this cultural belief, and this confusion prevents us from even knowing the next level exists!

How many of you love only those people who behave in ways which you find acceptable? The idea that we can't be loved spontaneously, whether or not we do something, is inconsistent with our own personal experience of loving. Most of us love people who are as far from our standards of perfection as they can get. Yet we persist in the delusion that we are not equally as lovable, with our faults, as the next person.

We love others, when we are capable of it, because we feel good as a result of that loving. We love each other because we are all children of the same Creator, and because we are in this boat together. We love people because they are beautiful. We do not love people because they are perfect. We know this, yet we forget it often. We especially forget, when we fail to treat ourselves the way we treat others, with common courtesy.

One of the first things I noticed when I first read the twelve steps of Alcoholics Anonymous was that only the first step mentioned alcohol. All the other steps trained us to be loving people. They taught us how to remove barriers to being loved by others also, but there is nothing in those steps about manipulating others to love us. In fact, there is nothing in any of the twelve-step programs which teaches about manipulation. Instead, we are taught to be moral, spiritual, and honest. We are also constantly reminded that we will need to be abstinent from our addictions to be any of those things. All these principles work.

## Fear of Love

There is a simple way of knowing whether we are being truly loving. If we are feeling fear, in any form, we can't be feeling love at the same time. A desire for either security, sensation, or power will always have some level of fear at its foundation. We merely need to learn to recognize it. The question can always be whether we are feeling unconditional love towards ourselves and others or we are feeling obvious or subtle fear. If we are feeling fear, we are not moving in the direction of learning to be happy.

I can easily give examples of confusing love and fear. When our children are ill and we feel a sense of panic, that is fear, not love. The panic is based on our fear of losing the child, not on our love. At times when we feel this way, we put a strain on our children by overprotective behavior which we mistakenly think is loving. When this type of behavior occurs habitually, it becomes the worrying addiction mentioned before.

When we feel that our spouses may be interested in someone else, the feelings of rage, jealousy, and panic are not based on love, nor are they love itself. They are merely fear that we will lose our secure relationship with this person. If we act on these panic feelings, we do not act very lovable, and the fear can produce a *self-fulfilling prophecy*. When we finally meet someone we think is a good prospect for a stable relationship, the feelings of longing for them and of fear that they will not want us are definitely not love. They may entail lust, but not love. Unfortunately, we are taught that they do, and marry people on the basis of our fear of being unlovable.

We are loving when our child is ill, and we ask them what they need, and radiate love as we provide for those needs and leave them alone when they need to be left alone.

We are loving when we think someone we love is interested in someone else, and are able to discuss it with them with the idea in mind that their happiness is important to us. We also act more lovable, and remind them why they chose us in the first place.

We are loving when we find that we have developed a friendship over a period of time with someone which means we would prefer to share the adventure of life with them. We know that they love us and that we love them. We have no need for fear in this interaction.

The last examples are of people who have learned to love as a high priority. We are often faced with the choice to feel love or fear. It is a matter of priorities. Love allows us freedom and moves us ahead to happier resolutions of problems. Fear causes us to become rigid and to try to make life static and the servant of our wishes.

We can learn to love more unconditionally through self-help programs, some religious organizations, close friendships, marriages, and families. While it is difficult, but possible, to learn unconditional love through a courting relationship, it is better to develop the skills in other relationships first. This is consistent with the self-help philosophy of avoiding emotionally entangling relationships (romantic ones) for at least the first year of recovery. We will find it too easy to switch our current addiction to one with another addicted person.

### Competence

One of my first premises was that addiction was an incompetent coping style, that while it appeared to be rational to the addict, it was, in fact, insane. I hope that the reader accepts that at this point. So far, in this chapter, we have stated that we need to be able to love others in building a better model of reality. These factors are the philosophical foundation for the action part of recovery, developing a competent coping style.

My definition of competence has developed over the past four or five years as I have worked with a premise developed by Richard Bandler and John Grinder in their book, *Frogs into Princes*. In this book, they stated that when we only have one coping option, we are puppets. When we only have two, we are robots. We need three or more options in order to be human.

Let us review the original addictive coping model:

| Problem | Symptom | Treatment |
|---------|---------|-----------|
| *Bad marriage* | *Anxiety* | *Drink* |

This person is a puppet if he is alcoholic. There are obviously other options, but he doesn't see them.

There are always at least three options in any situation of this nature. The first we will consider is the addictive one. This option solves nothing and eventually creates new problems. The second, and obvious option, is to seek to solve the problem. The third, for those in self-help programs, is to "turn it over," meaning to do nothing and let God lead you. There are usually more than these three options, but the addict, because of the addiction, only sees one. In the chapter on focusing and the addictive complex, I pointed out that people like to keep three addictive options in their addictive complexes. This serves to give a broader feeling to their coping options and allows the illusion of having several options. In reality, there is only one option, treatment of feelings. This single option is merely acted out in three or more ways.

Addictive behavior falls into the broad category of behavior known as compulsions. Compulsions are behaviors used habitually in coping situations, without regard for potential outcomes. The person following a compulsion does not consider alternatives to the compulsive behavior. Cigarette smoking is an excellent example of compulsive behavior. So is habitual lying. They have much in common with other addictive behaviors.

In my experience, one key to combating compulsive behaviors is to slow them down! In order for a compulsion to work, it must happen fast, and in a circular manner. The person's mind must present him with one alternative and only one alternative for behavior and he must follow this behavior quickly. This is puppet-like behavior. We become puppets to a part of our own minds.

So one rule of thumb is: do nothing until you have considered at least three alternatives, two of which are not fix-oriented. It is preferable to consider at least five. One of these alternatives is to do nothing. This is an excellent way of slowing things down. We often need to walk away, or distance ourselves in some way, from stimulus in order to do this effectively. If you begin rehearsing situations in advance and consider the non-addictive responses before you are faced with a choice, you will find yourself more successful.

There are three aspects of successful coping styles; rationality, flexibility, and farsightedness. Addiction is irrational, rigid, and shortsighted. By generating more than one option, you increase the probability of developing rationality and flexibility, especially if you base your analysis on the recovery core-beliefs. Farsightedness requires more thought.

How does one develop farsightedness and live one-day-at-a-time? Very carefully. Kenneth Keyes suggests that we plan as needed to be successful, but to stay unattached to the outcomes of the plans. This approach works, but will take some time for the newly recovering person to master. We can work with a therapist and a sponsor in this area. The development of farsightedness in the coping style of a newly recovering person will take time, about two years.

Finally, there is an organizing idea which is the most important idea of this part of recovery. The most important thing to develop in your model of reality and coping strategies is a sense of balance. All things in moderation is one key, but all things in balance is a better one. There are acronyms in the self-help groups which help you to maintain this balance, such as *K.I.S.S.* (Keep It Simple Stupid), *H.A.L.T.* (Don't get too Hungry, Angry, Lonely, or Tired), as well as others. These types of statements are quite helpful.

The realization of the need for balance has been one of the consistent themes in the addiction field in the past few years. Where we used to send recovering alcoholics to "ninety meetings in ninety days" on a regular basis, we now balance such recommendations against the needs of family and work. We recommend changes in diet and exercise and caution clients against simply switching to a work addiction to fill their need for time structure. We involve the whole family in attempts to create balance in the entire family system as soon as possible. This trend is sure to continue because it is obvious that it works well.

I have covered some of the most important points of building a better model of reality and dealing with it effectively as you try to recover from addictive coping. I encourage you, again, to get involved with others in pursuing these objectives.

*For Your Personal Growth*

*Review a particularly persistent problem in your life. How many alternatives do you usually consider when tackling it? Are any of them addictive? Have any of them worked?*

*List several problems and brainstorm several alternatives for each of them. Include in this list the option of turning each problem over to God. Notice how your feelings change as you view all those alternatives.*

# PUTTING IT ALL
# TOGETHER

*Life is difficult.*
- M. Scott Peck

This book has proposed a model of addictive process which covers many aspects of the subject. I have defined addictive process, charted its development, and described the different addictions people develop. I have outlined how enhancement behaviors can develop into addictive disease. I expanded the concept of progression by talking about how addictions fit together over time by "focusing" into "complexes." We explored how our addictions complement those of others in our lives. And we have also looked at the place of addictive behavior in the overall scheme of human growth and development.

After covering the addictive process, I presented two stages of the recovery process. The recovery steps which were described in detail are consistent with most treatment programs for addictions and with the twelve-step programs which are helping so many addicts today.

Now, let's go beyond the idea of recovery, and finish by moving into some ideas about living healthy lives, adding to our stability, reducing our distress and maintaining a high level of both physical and mental health. These ideas are not just about rebuilding maps of reality, they are about developing stable, happy lives.

As I have used the metaphor of maps or models of reality several times during this volume, it is important to describe how the core belief of recovery is integrated into healthy lives and how to know what we must do if we are to complete recovery and build a meaningful life.

One of the problems in this effort is that very few people have done studies of well people. Most models of health are based on conjecture. This leaves us with a problem in that some of the descriptions of health, especially descriptions in the literature of healthy families, may not exist except in the describer's fantasies.

Luckily, there is a relatively new science of *salutogenesis*, developed by Antonovsky and others, which studies well people and looks for common elements in their lives. Without this science, the model presented here would also be conjecture. For the brave among you, I recommend Antonovsky's *Health, Stress, and Coping*, a difficult book but one filled with much information.

From his model of wellness and the preceding model of addictive behavior, here are some summary guidelines to use as you continue building your new life. This model stresses again that abstinence is only the beginning of what is necessary for recovery. This is a description of the road beyond recovery for most of you. As such, it should help you stretch your thinking.

### Recovery Core Beliefs

I have referred throughout to the core beliefs of addiction and of recovery, and as we are now concerned with expanded recovery, I will review the core beliefs which we need to develop to move further ahead into health:

*Completely integrate the core belief that happiness is something which results from the love returned from those whom one loves without reservation or condition, from the emotional acceptance of one's beauty, capability and lovability, and from the acceptance of, and gratefulness for, one's actual place in the universe.*

This is a very tall order for most and requires that we make what Lew Presnall called in his 1959 book *Search For Serenity,* "our utmost effort to join the human race." This is difficult for anyone convinced that the world is hostile, and this is certainly difficult for the addict.

This type of growth, however, is necessary in order for us to achieve the continued peace of mind to which recovering people refer. This philosophy is a statement of interdependence with all things, and reflects Hall's *Prophet* stage of values. It is a worthy goal for us to achieve.

In working towards this core belief, we need to expand our perspective from a problem-solving viewpoint, which is necessary in early recovery, to a growth perspective. The early recovery is the foundation for the rest of our lives. We need to go on and build the rest of the structure. To continue is both desirable and necessary.

This continued growth is necessary because once we have developed an addiction, that addiction will always remain on our coping menus. If we do not continue to keep more desirable items on the menu, we will be likely to return to the addictive choice. Recovery never ends.

The growth is also desirable because such growth is part of our natural developmental process and adds to the happiness and meaning in our lives. As addiction is an unnatural process, the process of maturation is a natural process. Once we have developed power-level addictions, we only have the options of going forward or backwards. Our internal desire for our addictions will always act as a force pulling us backwards into our previous fear-based reality. It is an emotional handicap which we must constantly battle to overcome. For those who continue this struggle, the addiction is often the greatest blessing in their lives. Many people have found happiness in recovery which they probably would not have found without the motivating force of having to outgrow their addictions. There are some practical parts of maintaining this healthy growth which we need to address.

## Positive Social Supports and Ties

The development of social supports needs to start with other recovering people and expand over time to include others who are not struggling with major addictions. We need to build a social network and each of us is responsible for building one for ourselves. It needs to continue until we feel we have completely rejoined the human race. We need to learn to work and play with others in happy, loving ways. After we have learned to do this, we need to persist at it.

## Committed Relationships

The committed relationship is a vital support for growth. This doesn't have to be a romantic relationship, in fact it can't be for many of us, at least during early recovery. It is a relationship in which two or more people commit to honesty and supportiveness of each other's growth and development. It is an intimate relationship in which feelings can be safely shared. The essential ingredients here are commitment and unconditional loving. We each need to feel that someone loves us unconditionally. In order for this to happen, we need to commit to those we love that we will continue to love them, regardless of short-term friction. We do not have to like the behaviors of those we love, but commitment is the single most important force in learning to love.

As I stated earlier, this doesn't have to be a romantic relationship. I have a few of these intimate relationships (no one can manage several of them), and they provide much of the joy in my life. Only one of the relationships is my marriage. Intimacy and romance go together well, but they are not the same things.

## Ability to Maintain Loving Relationships

This ability comprises a set of committing, listening, sharing, and nurturing skills which nurture the growth of others. One develops this ability by practicing the maintenance of the committed relationships just mentioned. It also requires the practice of constant forgiveness described in an earlier chapter. When we realize that almost all our conflict with others comes from our attempts to have the control we want in our lives, it is easier to "own" our part of conflict. The steps of doing an ongoing inventory and forgiving the illusion that anyone is harming us when they refuse to cater to us is an incredibly powerful tool in maintaining close relationships.

## Committed Spirituality

In order to benefit from spirituality, make a commitment to taking advantage of the stable set of answers which the spiritual belief system offers. Discover what answers are available within AA, churches, and other groups of people seeking an escape from rational madness, and explore the beliefs generated within those groups. This is a difficult balance to maintain, and one must be sure that this is a group, church, or other activity in which the stable answers are loving and truly work. This will allow you to reduce the amount of time spent in trying to be God and increases the amount of time available for developing spirituality. The development of a self-image founded on a spiritual base releases fear and allows love to flourish. Creating this self-image will require participation in a spiritual program with others because such an image conflicts with much of the society at large.

## Rational, Flexible, and Farsighted Strategy

Antonovsky stresses that each of us must have a rational, flexible, and farsighted coping strategy in order to maintain mental and physical health. The key to this strategy is to follow a path that works and has a probability of continuing to work. If we find that a chosen path doesn't work, we need to change our strategy. This flexible approach to reality will make it easier to redraw our maps when necessary and will allow us to grow. We addressed this issue in more depth earlier when we explored coping competence.

## Material Stability

Being broke is stressful. We can be broke because we over-spend or we can be broke because we do not produce adequate income for our needs. We need to work with others in assessing our real needs, separate them from our wants, and plan to assure that our real needs of food, clothing, and shelter are met. We will want to go beyond that point, but we need to seek continuous feedback from others in our support groups about whether we are creating needless stress over financial matters. We need to keep stress in this area at a minimum.

If we do not have skills which allow us to adequately provide us with the material stability we need, we need to develop those skills through schooling, on-the-job training, or some other means of skill development. We are responsible for our own salvation. We are also responsible for our own support. The developmental process of going from dependence to independence to inter-dependence also holds true in the financial area of our lives. Being financially dependent on others interferes with our dealing with them on an equal footing.

## Adequate Intelligence and Knowledge

In order to do something right, you must know how. This requires two things, intelligence and information. Our intelligence levels vary and we all have a finite limit on how much we can know. Very few of us, however, even come close to that limit and it is seldom necessary to do so. Some of us do have limits on our abilities to learn, but this isn't relevant to recovery.

While practicing our addictions, most of us fail to try com-petent methods of coping, then blame the world because we fail. This is an important thing to change. The addict stays ignorant as a part of his strategy to keep from admitting he is wrong. We owe it to ourselves to develop a knowledge base which allows us to be both emotionally and financially stable. For those of us who have the capacity to learn, to do otherwise is insane.

## Genetic Makeup

This book has stressed that genetic differences are important in addiction. We all have different genetic potentials. Alcoholism and obesity are just two of the health problems linked to genetics. We all need to learn to deal rationally with our genetic blocks to health and serenity. A few of us have even inherited fatal diseases which do not relate to addictions. In any case, we all need to play the game of life reasonably well with the cards we are dealt.

## Persistence

An important part of any change program is persistence. There is a line in the AA "Big Book" which starts, "Rarely have we seen it fail . . . " The idea is that if one applies oneself to the AA program on a persistent and consistent basis, success is almost inevitable. This is also true of the suggestions in this volume.

The problem most encountered, even when a person knows he has a problem, with following any recovery program is one of unjustified conceit over one's current coping mechanisms. Most people defend their current coping methods regardless of the success which they achieve. This is true of people with any and all addictions. Most of us have difficulty admitting that we need help. *It is even more difficult to admit that we need help to understand what help we need.* When we have false confidence in poor coping mechanisms, we deny the need to ask for anything.

Most addictions counselors have years of experience of sending people to Alcoholics Anonymous, Narcotics Anonymous, and Overeaters Anonymous, only to have them come back and say they "didn't like it." Then we have difficulty in getting them to go back.

As children, many of us learned that medicine was not necessarily supposed to taste good. If we were extremely ill, we didn't care. With most addicts, obsessed as they are with avoidance of pain, the idea that they need to do some things which may be unpleasant at first is often insulting to them. In spite of a lifetime of failure at being happy and a spoken admission of this, they still have difficulty believing in their incompetence in this area. This is true in every addiction.

For those of you who are already living a serene life with no addictions, I hope you have been reinforced in your lifestyle by reading this book. I also hope you have gained some ideas which might be useful in enjoying your lives even more than you do now.

For others who are not so fortunate, if you have recognized addictions in yourself, persistence will be your most important issue after putting down this book. You will have difficulty following the recommended steps. One of the first lessons in recovery is that we can't do it alone, and this irritates the self-centered, conceited ego of the addict. With help, you can overcome this obstacle.

If you can, find a therapist and self-help group as soon as possible. If you have one or more addictions, and have read this far, there is a chink in your armor. If you wait, it will repair itself.

Begin working with others in learning to see reality in new ways, in learning new lessons, and in fostering relaxed, healthy feelings. This will take time and effort, but far less time and effort than you would spend trying to cope by the incompetent means of your addictions.

Continue to read. Involve as many family members as possible in the recovery process because they are addicts too. Dedicate your energies to being happy for a change.

There are many sources of help available. Unfortunately, some of them are quite expensive, and beyond the reach of some of our budgets. Self-help groups are almost free and available to all.

Most importantly, "*Act!*" Begin to do things differently and keep at it. Follow the lead of others who have been successful and copy them. It works. To do otherwise is to let yourself down. After all, all you have to lose is your madness.

# NOTES ON SOURCES

There are many authors and co-workers whose ideas have contributed to this book. While it is impossible to give credit to everyone whose ideas have influenced my work, I have tried to cite the major influences on the development of my own perspective. I hope this effort gives you the basis for a broader insight into the the models presented here.

## PROLOGUE

2    SOON, I DISCOVERED    Keyes and Hatterer offer, respectively, a spiritual and psychiatric perspective on addiction. Each was helpful for the range of personal issues I faced.    Kenneth Keyes, *Handbook to Higher Consciousness* (St. Mary, KY: Living Love Publications, 1978).    Lawrence Hatterer, *The Pleasure Addicts* (South Brunswick, NJ: A.S. Barnes, 1989).

## INTRODUCTION

5    "WHAT WE LIVE..."    The epigraph is a statement often used in addictions work. I attribute it to Larsen because I've seen it in his writings and been exposed to it in his workshops more than in other sources.    Earnie Larsen, *Stage II Relationships* (New York, NY: Harper & Row, 1987); and *Stage II Recovery: Life Beyond Addiction* (Harper & Row, 1985).

8    HATTERER, IN "THE PLEASURE..."  At first, I found this insight of Hatterer's profound. Later, I realized that it was intensity of experience, not pleasure of experience which was most important. An experience may be intense, but not really pleasurable at all and nevertheless lead to addiction.

8    I FIRST BEGAN  Dr. Glenn added a great deal to my early understanding of addictions. His work in developing the audiotape "Creating Chemically Independent Children" (Indianapolis, IN: Access, 1985) is some of the most effective works being done in the area of drug abuse prevention.  Stephen Glenn, *Raising Children For Success* (Fair Oaks, CA: Sunrise Press, 1987).

11   ONE OF THE MAJOR  Kenneth Keyes describes security, sensation, and power as the primary outcomes of addictions. He sees addictions as "emotion-backed-demands" for these three outcomes. He also states that experience in these three areas is necessary in order for us to achieve higher, more mature states of consciousness. In this sense, addictive demands can be seen as developmentally necessary.

11   ADDICTIVE COPING PATTERNS  In theme 1, for a more complete description, I suggest *When Society Becomes An Addict* by Anne Wilson-Schaef (New York, NY: Harper & Row, 1987); and *Co-dependence: Misunderstood-Mistreated* (Minneapolis, MN: Winston Press, 1986).

11   FOR EACH INDIVIDUAL  In theme 2, I suggest study of the forty or more publications on Neuro-Linguistic Programming. The concept of modeling is completely described in this literature.

12   A MAJOR DISTORTION  In theme 3, I again suggest Wilson-Schaef's book *When Society Becomes An Addict*.

12   THERE ARE SEVERAL  In theme 4, I suggest any of Wilson-Schaef's writings, as well as the writings of Patrick Carnes, *Out Of The Shadows* (Minneapolis, MN: CompCare Publications, 1983); and *Counseling The Sexual Addict* (Compcare Publications, 1984).

12   ADDICTIONS BECOME FOCUSED   The "addictive complex" is my description of this phenomenon, but Patrick Carnes says a very similar thing when he states that addictions come in "families." Another author addressed this grouping of addictions as addictive "snarls." I particularly like the use of "snarls" as a descriptive term here.

12   THERE ARE PREDICTABLE   This idea of predictable patterns is covered in many books on "co-dependence." I also suggest reviewing Robert Ackerman's *Children Of Alcoholics: A Guide for Parents* (Holmes Beach, FL: Learning Publications, 1987). A particularly good autobiographical work is *Potato Chips For Breakfast* by Cynthia Scales (Rockaway, NJ: Quotidian Press, 1986).

13   ADDICTIVE BEHAVIOR IS   Theme 9 is my interpretation of the widespread recognition of retarded emotional maturity demonstrated by addicts in treatment. The ideas for this were probably first generated by a speech by Dr. Brian Hall in the early 1970's. It was easy to see how Dr. Hall's, Erik Erikson's and Kohlberg's description of developmental stages were distorted by my clients in their process of addiction. The addictive process seemed to supplant the developmental process until recovery occurred.   Brian Hall, *The Development Of Consciousness* (Ramsey, NJ: Paulist Press, 1976).   Laurence Kohlberg, *The Philosophy Of Moral Development* (San Francisco, CA: Harper & Row, 1981).   Erik Erickson, *Vital Involvement In Old Age* (New York, NY: W.W. Norton And Son, 1986); *Childhood And Society* (1985); *The Life Cycle Completed, A Review* (W.W. Norton, 1982); *Identity And The Life Cycle* (W. W. Norton, 1980); and *Adulthood* (W. W. Norton, 1978).

13   AS BANDLER AND   For Bandler and Grinder's description, see *The Structure Of Magic* (Palo Alto, CA: Science And Behavior Books, 1975). I also suggest *Frogs Into Princes* (Moab, UT: Real People Press, 1979) by the same authors for further expansion of this concept.

## ADDICTION IN SOCIETY

15    IF WE LOVE   Wilson-Schaef's premise is very consistent with the theme of this chapter.

16    AARON ANTONOVSKY, IN   Antonovsky is an Israeli researcher in the field of "salutogenesis," the study of why healthy people stay that way. Aaron Antonovsky, *Health, Stress, And Coping* (San Francisco, CA: Jossey-Bass, 1979).

16    TO PARAPHRASE HERB   In *The Hazards Of Being Male* (New York, NY: Nash Publications, 1976), *The New Male* (New York, NY: New American Library, 1979), and *The New Male-Female Relationship* (New York, NY: New American Library, 1983), Mr. Goldberg makes a strong case for this point of view. I also recommend *Transitions, Making Sense Of Life's Changes* by William Bridges (Reading, MA: Addison-Wesley, 1980).

17    THE "MAGIC" ANSWERS   Antonovsky credits culture with providing the "magic" answers which we have at our disposal, but which usually remain outside of conscious awareness.

19    ADDICTIVE BEHAVIORS ARE   See Patrick Carnes' *Out Of The Shadows* (Minneapolis, MN: Compcare Publications, 1983) for an understanding of the power of rituals as it relates to sexual addiction.

20    WHEN WE DISCOVER   In Steve Glenn's work, he emphasizes the power of identification with a role model and its effect on addiction.

23    FOR MY PART   See early studies by Bales, R. F. "Cultural differences in the rates of alcoholism" *Q.J. Stud. Alcohol* 6:480-499, 1946; Snyder, C. R. *Alcohol and The Jews: A Cultural Study of Drinking and Sobriety* (Glencoe, Il: Free Press, 1958). An extensive bibliograpy of sources on cultural variations associated with patterns of alcohol use is Heath, D. B. and Cooper, A. M. *Alcohol Use and World Cultures: A Comprehensive Bibliography of Anthropological Sources* (Toronto, Canada: Addiction Research Foundation, 1981).

23    ERIKSON, MASLOW, KOHLBERG  All these authors
       are valuable sources for understanding human growth and
       development. The works of Erik Erikson are perhaps the
       best known and most comprehensive. Abraham Maslow,
       *The Farther Reaches Of Human Nature* (New York, NY:
       Viking Press, 1971).

25    OUR MODELS OF  For a more complete description of
       the addictive nature of "romantic love," I recommend
       *Co-Dependence: Misunderstood-Mistreated* by Anne
       Wilson-Schaef (Minneapolis, MN: Winston Press, 1986).

28    WHEN DADDY'S AN  The works of Robert Ackerman,
       Janet Woititz, Sharon Wegscheider, Claudia Black and
       several others note the relatively high probability of
       children of alcoholics becoming alcoholics. Janet Woititz,
       *Home Away From Home* (Deerfield Beach, FL: Health
       Communications, 1987); and *Struggle For Intimacy* (Health
       Communications, 1985).  Sharon Wegscheider, *Another
       Chance, Hope And Health For The Alcoholic Family* (Palo
       Alto, CA: Science And Behavior Books, 1981); and
       *Choice-Making* (Health Communications, 1985).  Claudia
       Black, *It Will Never Happen To Me* (Denver, CO: M.A.C.,
       1981).

29    ONE OF THE  There have been several studies which
       indicate that tendencies to be alcoholic or obese seem to
       occur at the same statistical frequency in children of
       addicts raised in situations in which they never knew their
       biological parents as in those raised in their biological
       families. The most impressive research seems to be going
       on within Swedish universities.

## MAPS, POWERLESSNESS AND CONTROL

33    "NONE OF US..."  The epigraph comes from *Stage II
       Recovery*, p. 43. It reflects Larsen's understanding of the
       subjective nature of our experience.

34    THE IDEA OF PEOPLE  For a more complete descrip-
       tion of these ideas, I recommend reading *The Structure Of
       Magic, volumes I and II*, by Richard Bandler and John

Grinder (Palo Alto, CA: Science And Behavior Books, 1975).

34   MOST OF US   Without the prior development of *Neuro-Linguistic Programming*, by Bandler, Grinder, and others, this book probably would not have had the scope it has. This science helped me learn to think "relatively" in therapy and helped me see the interrelationships between many factors described here.

36   ONE WAY IS   Deletion, distortion, and generalization are covered in depth in *The Structure Of Magic*, volumes I & II.

37   ORGANIC VERSUS MACHINELIKE   This conflict between organic and machinelike views of man is described by Herb Goldberg in *The Hazards Of Being Male; The New Male; and The New Male/Female Relationship*; and William Bridges in *Transitions*. Both address the concept of growth and development being organic processes which our society has few models to explain.

39   CORE BELIEFS OF   The most notable work being done with core beliefs is that of Patrick Carnes and his associates in Minnesota. They have identified core beliefs of sexual addicts. I have attempted to go further in the direction indicated by their work.

40   GOING THE WRONG   Regarding the differences in belief systems mentioned here, Viktor Frankl talks about these in *Man's Search For Meaning* (Boston, MA: Beacon Press, 1959) and in his works on *Logotherapy*. Lew Presnall, in his classic *Search For Serenity* (Salt Lake City, UT: U.A.F., 1959), makes points very similar to the ones here. All three of us describe growth as moving from the self-centered belief systems to the more balanced loving world view.

42   ."..NAMELY THE FEELING..."   *Man's Search For Meaning*, p. 128

42   "THE VOID" IS   In spite of the parallels with Frankl's work and my description of the "void," I only discovered Frankl's work while looking for sources to corroborate my

proposal of this feeling. I suggest reading Frankl's works for a deeper understanding of this phenomenon.

43    THE OTHER FEELING    I have found no other descriptions of the "nova," but the restlessness that preceeds some addictive behavior, and especially relapse, is well-documented. This feeling is at the center of the problems of the alcoholics who relapse because they "can't stand prosperity."

43    "MOREOVER, THERE ARE..." *Man's Search for Meaning*, p. 129-130.

44    AS SUCH, IT    C.C. Nuckols states in his tapes on cocaine and other polydrug abuse that addiction occurs in trance. Patrick Carnes provides an excellent example in *Out Of The Shadows* of the trance state of a "cruising" sex addict who follows a woman who he thinks is flirting with him to the police station before he realizes that the look on her face is fear, not interest. C.C. Nuckols, *Understanding And Treating Cocaine Addiction* (Indianapolis, IN: Access, 1985); *Current Issues In Cocaine Treatment* (Access, 1988); *Crack And Rock* (Access, 1986); *Understanding And Treating The Dual Diagnosis Patient* (Access, 1985); *Advanced Strategies For Treating Cocaine Addiction* (Access, 1987); and his book, *Cocaine: From Dependency To Recovery* (Bradenton, FL: Human Services Institute, 1987).

46    IN HER BOOK    Shakti Gawain is a "New Age" writer who is popular with several of my recovering friends. Her ideas of spiritual growth are quite consistent with self-help principles. Shakti Gawain, *Living In The Light* (Mill Valley, CA: Whatever Publications, 1986).

51    THE CHOICE SEEMS    Richard Bandler, *Using Your Brain For A Change* (Moab, UT: Real People Press, 1985).

52    FEELINGS ARE NOT    For further descriptions of how emotions change in response to thoughts, I suggest *The Emotional Hostage* by Leslie Cameron-Bandler and Michael Lebeau (San Rafael, CA: FuturePace, Inc., 1986). This book offers healthy, non-addictive techniques for

producing appropriate emotional responses to situations in our lives.

## RELATIONSHIPS AND ADDICTION

55   "HEALTHY PEOPLE HAVE..."  Epigraph is from *Stage II Relationships* by Earnie Larsen.

57   ME, YOU, AND GOD  For an elegant discussion of the relationship between our intrapersonal, interpersonal and spiritual relationips, I suggest *The Road Less Traveled* by M. Scott Peck (New York, NY: Simon and Schuster, 1978).

58   IN SHORT, THE  This idea of "systematic suicide" comes from Lee Silverstein. He presented this idea in a workshop I attended several years ago; he has several publications. Anne Wilson-Schaef has also stated that the real addiction is to powerlessness and death.

61   MY APPROACH IS  Anne Wilson-Schaef goes into detail on large group co-dependence in *Co-Dependence: Misunderstood, Mistreated.*

61   "THE DENIAL OR..."  Robert Subby, *Lost In The Shuffle* (Deerfield Beach, FL: Health Communications, 1987).

62   THERE IS A CONSTANT  Herbert Goldberg documents this power struggle in *The New Male/Female Relationship.*

63   "AN ADDICTIVE RELATIONSHIP..."  *When Society Becomes An Addict,* p. 26.

63   DRS. COWAN AND KINDER  Cowan and Kinder describe a relationship addiction in this book. Connel Cowan and Melvyn Kinder, *Smart Women Foolish Choices* (New York, NY: Signet, 1985).

64   THE ANGER OF  The point about the family's resentment at not being at the center of the addict's universe is discussed by Lew Presnall in *Search For Serenity.*

66   ADDICTION IS CONTAGIOUS  I first heard this "Addiction is contagious" statement from Patrick Carnes.

66   THE CHILDREN OF  The most complete research I have seen on the effects of growing up in addictive homes,

in this case alcoholic homes, was by Robert Ackerman. I recommend his books to the reader.

## THE ADDICTIONS

73    ADDICTIONS ARE NOT    The epigraph is from *Handbook To Higher Consciousness*, p. 20.

73    OTHER AUTHORS SUCH    Wilson-Schaef has a very complete discussion of the issues in this chapter in *When Society Becomes An Addict*. I have adopted some of her categories because they are extremely well thought-out.

74    WORK ADDICTION    There has been very little comprehensive research in the area of work addiction. One of the most comprehensive studies, published in *Workaholics: Living With Them, Working With Them*, by Marilyn Machlowitz (New York, NY: The New American Library, 1980) chronicles the disadvantages of such an addiction, then does little to confront the need for change. Machlowitz studied primarily successful work addicts who had high payoffs. Some of my most difficult work has been with workaholics who were unsuccessful.

74    THE FOLLOWING STORY    Dr. Jay B. Rohrlich, *Work and Love: The Crucial Balance* (New York: Summit Books, 1980).

77    WORK ADDICTION IS    Another recent societal development which reinforces this addiction has been the popularity of books such as *In Search Of Excellence* by Thomas Peters (New York, NY: Harper & Row, 1982), in which organizations which promote work, over family and other needs, for its employees are touted as examples for others to follow. The workaholic is beginning to be recognized as an addict, but the successful workaholic is still our cultural hero.

77    RELIGION ADDICTION    *Stage II Recovery*.

78    "RELIGION CAN ALSO..."    *When Society Becomes an Addict*, p. 23.

83    THE "BAD" ADDICTIONS    Again, the categories here parallel the categories in *When Society Becomes An Addict*.

84    WE NOW RECOGNIZE    Ackerman, Woititz, Weg-
      scheider, Black, Subby, and others have made adult
      children of alcoholics one of the most written-about
      groups in the country. Self-help groups have been develop-
      ed for this population.

85    FATHER JOSEPH MARTIN    Father Joseph Martin,
      from the film "Attitudes" (Los Angeles, CA: FMS Produc-
      tions, 1975).

85    WE GIVE GREAT    Since the writing of this book, I
      have begun to see inpatient treatment centers for the
      nicotine addicted. This is an exciting change.

87    COCAINE ADDICTION IS    For an in-depth discussion
      of the power of cocaine and cocaine addiction, I recom-
      mend *Cocaine: From Dependency To Recovery* by C.C.
      Nuckols (Human Services Insitute, 1987).

88    THE PERSON WHO    Those interested in learning more
      about food addiction could benefit from attending an open
      meeting of Overeaters Anonymous. Their literature is also
      quite good.

89    SEX ADDICTION    For those interested in sex addiction,
      I recommend *Out Of The Shadows* and *Counseling The
      Sexual Addict* by Patrick Carnes.

## ADDICTIVE BEHAVIOR AND PROCESS

95    "THE ADDICTIVE PROCESS"    *Co-Dependence:
      Misunderstood-Mistreated*, p.21.

97    HATTERER DEFINES ADDICTION    *The Pleasure
      Addicts*.

97    ON THE OTHER HAND    *Handbook to Higher Con-
      sciousness*.

97    ANNE WILSON-SCHAEF    *Co-Dependence: Misunder-
      stood-Mistreated; When Society Becomes an Addict*.

99    THESE SYMPTOMS ARE    This is a rephrasing of a
      passage in Howard M. Halpern, *How To Break Your
      Addiction To A Person* (New York, NY: Bantam Books,
      1982). His description of addiction is accurate for all
      addictions.

101    POST-ACUTE WITHDRAWAL   For detailed descriptions of Post-Acute Withdrawal, I refer the reader to the works of Jan Black, Terence Gorski, and Daniel McEachern, "Post-Acute Withdrawal: Recognition" (video part I) (Phoenix, AZ: Max Media); and "Post-Acute-Withdrawal: Management" (video part II) (Max Media).

## PROGRESSION

109    THE ADDICTIVE PROCESS   In the alcoholism research, the work of Jellinek and others pioneered this concept in the 1950's.

113    VIKTOR FRANKL   *Man's Search For Meaning*.

## FOCUSING

129    ADDICTIVE COPING IS   *Health, Stress, And Coping*.

## COMPLEMENTARY ADDICTIVE RELATIONSHIPS

137    "AN ALCOHOLIC SYSTEM"   *When Society Becomes An Addict*.

137    HATTERER DESCRIBED THE   *The Pleasure Addicts*.

138    PATRICK CARNES DESCRIBED THIS   Patrick Carnes, lecture, 1988, Indianapolis, Indiana.

138    IN MY VIEW   My views on co-dependents and victims seem to be shared by Robert Subby in *Lost In The Shuffle*.

143    THE CHILDREN'S PATTERNS   For descriptions of family, I recommend Sharon Wegcheiders works, especially *Another Chance*.

## THE TERRITORY

149    "OUR EXPERIENCE HAS..."   *The Structure Of Magic*, p.13. Bandler, Grinder, and others in the *Neuro-Linguistic Programming* hold that people are always doing the best they know how to do as a central belief to this model.

150    FOR SEVERAL YEARS    Gerald Jampolsky, *Love Is Letting Go Of Fear* (New York, NY: Bantam Books, 1970); *Teach Only Love* (Bantam Books, 1983); *Goodbye to Guilt* (Bantam Books, 1985).

151    ONE CAN LABEL    I owe the ideas of survival versus being consciousness to Brian Hall. He uses these terms in his various writings.

155    THE FOLLOWING IDEAS    Most of these theorists have several volumes on the ideas of human development. Each has his or her own perspective and I suggest that the reader review several authors if human development is an interest.

156    WHATEVER WE DO    A basic idea inherent in any discussion of human development is that of being a "hierarchical" species. Joe Yeager, in *Thinking About Thinking With NLP* (Cupertino, CA: Meta Publications, 1985), describes humans as "hierarchical mamals." The way we create hierarchies seems to be at the core of all human societies, and also, at the core of the process of "human development." Research on baboons and even Diane Fossey's work with gorillas shows hierarchical patterns in ape societies which parallel human patterns.

156    MOST DEVELOPMENTAL THEORISTS    Consistent in developmental research is the phenomenon of reduced emotional stress at higher levels of the developmental hierarchy. This pattern has also been duplicated in baboon research.

157    GIVEN WHAT WE KNOW    The stage descriptions here are integrations of ideas of Kenneth Keyes and Brian Hall. These theorists have the most flexibility in their models, in that they avoid predicting ages at which people will be at different stages.

160    FOR THE PERSON    In *Handbook to Higher Consciousness*, Keyes explains that the need for experience at the lower levels is necessary in order to grow into the higher levels of development.

## RECOVERY: THE NEW FRONTIER

163    "IF I HAD ONLY..."  *Notes To Myself* by Hugh Prather (Moab, UT: Real People Press, 1970).

165    FOR SEVERAL YEARS  For further reading, I suggest The "Big Book", *Alcoholics Anonymous* (New York, NY: Alcoholics Anonymous World Services, 1976), available at many bookstores and at local AA chapters..

167    THE ROAD AHEAD  "Stage I" and "Stage II" recovery are terminologies popularized by Earnie Larsen.

168    OTHERS HAVE TO  Perhaps the most significant ways of "raising one's bottom" are the intervention methods pioneered by The Johnson Institute in Minneapolis, Minnesota and popularized by its use with Betty Ford.

170    UNLESS THIS OCCURS  See the pamphlet *Twelve Steps And Twelve Traditions*, by Alcoholics Anonymous World Services, also available at many bookstores and at local AA chapters.

171    THIS WITHDRAWAL PAIN  This "Withdrawal Pain" is well described by Halpern in *How To Break Your Addiction To A Person*.

172    THE BEGINNING OF  For an excellent description of how this process works with chemicals, I suggest *Staying Sober, A Guide For Relapse Prevention* and *Staying Sober Workbook*, by Terence Gorski and Marlene Miller (Independence, MO: Independence Press, 1986).

## POWERLESSNESS

177    "WE CAME TO..."  This is the famous first step of Alcoholics Anonymous.

178    OUR TASK, INSTEAD  The reference to a "Power Greater Than Ourselves" is from the second step of the twelve-step recovery programs. The concept of trust in a "Higher Power" is from the third step of the twelve.

179    SINCE WORKING WITH  I worked with Dr. Stephen Glenn in 1972 and 1973. Both our approaches have expanded greatly since that time.

## ABSTINENCE

183  "ABSTINENCE AND THE..."  *Stage II Recovery*, p. 5

188  IN FOOD ADDICTION  Overeaters Anonymous and Weight Watchers are two organizations which probably hold meetings in your communities. OA is a self-help program based on the twelve steps and parallels Alcoholics Anonymous. Weight Watchers is a more behavioral program which teaches good eating habits and reinforces these habits on a weekly basis. Both are excellent organizations.

## SPIRITUALITY

195  "I BELIEVE THAT..."  *When Society Becomes an Addict*, p. 149.

196  AS M. SCOTT PECK  *The Road*, Chapter on "Growth And Religion."

197  THE HIGHER LEVELS  Brian Hall and Helen Thompson, in *Leadership Through Values*, (Ramsey, NJ: Paulist Press, 1980), describes their seventh stage as that of the "Prophet."

## THROWING OUT THE GARBAGE

201  "LOVE AND GUILT..."  This quote from "A Course In Miracles" makes the point that guilt is fear-based and interferes with loving. There is no author credited for this course which was published in 1975 by the Foundation For Inner Peace in Tiburon, CA.

205  KEN KEYES REFERS  *Handbook*, p.1.

## LEARNING FROM OTHERS

209  "WE ARE NOT..." From "A Course In Miracles," see note for page 201.

## ADVANCED RECOVERY

219    "DON'T AIM AT..."    *Man's Search For Meaning* (New York: Washington Square Press, 1959) pp. 16-17.

223    "I BELIEVE THAT..."   Earnie Larsen, *Stage II Recovery*, p.15.

225    THERE IS A    There are several excellent books on this subject written by Gerald Jampolsky, Kenneth Keyes, and others. As our societal level of awareness about love is changing, we are producing several wise works.

## PUTTING IT ALL TOGETHER

231    "LIFE IS DIFFICULT."   *The Road Less Traveled*, p.1.

233    THIS IS A VERY TALL    Lewis Presnall, *Search for Serenity* (Salt Lake City, UT: U.S. Air Force, 1959).

233    THIS TYPE OF GROWTH   *Leadership Through Values*. 1980.

# INDEX

# INDEX

I gratefully acknowledge permission which I have received to include material from the following copyrighted books and articles:

*Man's Search for Meaning* by Viktor E. Frankl, Copyright 1959, 1962, 1984 by Viktor E. Frankl. By permission of Beacon Press.

Excerpt p. 21 from *Co-Dependence: Misunderstood-Mistreated* by Anne Wilson-Schaef. Copyright 1986 by Anne Wilson-Schaef. Reprinted by permission of Harper & Row, Publishers, Inc.

Excerpt p. 5 and p. 43 from *Stage II Relationships* by Earnie Larsen. Copyright 1986 by Earnie Larsen. Reprinted by permission of Harper & Row, Publishers, Inc.

Excerpt pgs. 27-29 from *Work and Love: The Crucial Balance* by Jay Rohrlich, Copyright 1980 by Jay Rohrlich. Summit Books, Reprinted by permission of the author.

Excerpt p. 20 from *Handbook to Higher Consciousness* by Kenneth Keyes, Jr., Copyright 1978 by Kenneth Keys. Reprinted by permission of Living Love Publications.

Excerpt p. 1 from *Notes to Myself* by Hugh Prather, Copyright 1970 by Hugh Prather. Reprinted by permission of Real People Press.